CONCORDIA
CURRICULUM GUIDE

GRADE
8

Science

CONCORDIA PUBLISHING HOUSE · SAINT LOUIS

Copyright © 2007 Concordia Publishing House
3558 S. Jefferson Ave., St. Louis, MO 63118-3968
1-800-325-3040 • www.cph.org

Prepared with materials provided by Nathan Jastram, Julaine Kammrath, Karen Miller, Rodney Rathmann, Terry Umphenour, and John Weber

Edited by Rodney L. Rathmann

Science Consultant: Roy Pfund

Series editors: Carolyn Bergt, Clarence Berndt, and Rodney L. Rathmann

CONTENTS

PREFACE

Ministry of Christian Schools

Parental expectations of Christian schools include

- excellent discipline;
- high academic standards;
- low teacher-student ratios;
- dedicated, conscientious teachers.

Many Christian schools offer these advantages. But the real distinction is that Christian schools proclaim Jesus Christ as the Son of God and Savior of the world. Teaching Jesus Christ, then, is "the real difference" between Christian and public schools. In Christian schools, teachers and students witness personally and publicly to their faith in Jesus Christ. Students study the Bible and worship God daily. Teachers relate Jesus Christ to all aspects of the curriculum. Teachers and students share Christian love and forgiveness.

Those who teach in Christian schools are privileged with the opportunity to

- teach the Word of God in its truth and purity;
- acknowledge the Bible as God's infallible Word and the Confessions as the true exposition of the Word;
- identify God's Word, Baptism, and the Lord's Supper as the means through which God creates and sustains faith;
- emphasize Law and Gospel as the key teaching of Scripture;
- seek to apply Law and Gospel properly in daily relationships with students, parents, and other teachers;
- teach all of what Scripture teaches (including Christian doctrines) to all students, no matter what backgrounds they have;
- share with students what Jesus, the Savior, means to them personally;
- equip students to proclaim the Good News to others;

- encourage students to find the support and encouragement found only in the body of Christ, of which Jesus Himself is the head.

In Christian schools, Christ permeates all subjects and activities. Religion is not limited to one hour or one class. Teachers seek opportunities to witness in every class and to relate God's Word to all aspects of life. Through this process, and by the power of the Holy Spirit, students grow in faith and in a sanctified life, and view all of life, not just Sunday, as a time to serve and worship God.

In summary, it is intrinsic to ministry in a Christian school that all energies expended in the educational process lead each child to a closer relationship with the Savior and with other members of the Christian community.

How to Use This Guide

The Concordia Curriculum Guide series is designed to guide you as you plan and prepare to teach. The introductory chapters provide foundational information relevant to the teaching of science to students in a Christian school. But the majority of the pages in this volume focus on science standards and performance expectations together with ideas and activities for integrating them with various aspects of the Christian faith. This volume does not provide a curriculum plan or lesson plan for any particular period or day. Instead, it provides a wealth of ideas from which you can choose and a springboard to new ideas you may create. You may use this curriculum guide with any textbook series.

The science standards included in this book are informed by the Benchmarks for Science Literacy, published in conjunction with Project 2061 of the American Association for the Advancement of Science (AAAS) (see also ch. 3), and are provided as a compilation of the science standards and performance expectations adopted by the individual states. In order to offer a well-coordinated curriculum design, the science objectives for this grade level relate to and connect with the standards provided at other grade levels.

The standards, then, can serve you and your whole faculty in several ways. They can help you

1. plan your teaching in an organized way;

2. coordinate your teaching of a subject with the teaching in other grades in your school;

3. select textbooks and other learning or teaching materials;

4. evaluate your current instruction, materials, and objectives;

5. implement procedures for school accreditation;

6. nurture the Christian faith of your students as you teach science.

We assume that teachers will use materials in addition to those included in the guide, but, since many materials do not integrate the Christian faith, we have provided suggestions for specific methods to use as you teach day by day. Everyone has a different teaching style. No one will be able to use all the ideas in this volume. As you think about practices that will work for you and would be helpful in your classroom, consider these possible ways to find and use ideas from this volume:

• Read the entire volume before school starts. Highlight the ideas you think you can use.

• Write ideas in your textbooks. List the page numbers from this volume that contain suggestions you would like to use in connection with a lesson or unit.

• Throughout the year, designate periods of time, perhaps at faculty meetings, to discuss portions of this volume as you seek to improve your integration of the faith in science. Brainstorm, develop, and implement your ideas. Then follow up with other meetings to share your successes and challenges. Together, find ways to effectively use the suggestions in this volume.

• Plan ways to adapt ideas not closely related to specific lessons or units in your secular textbooks. Inside your plan book, clip a paper with a list of suggestions from the volume that you would like to use, or list each idea on a file card and keep the cards handy for quick review. Use those ideas between units or when extra time is available.

• Evaluate each suggestion after you have tried it. Label it as "use again" or "need to revise." Always adapt the suggestions to fit your situation.

• Think about integrating the faith each time you plan a lesson. Set a goal for yourself (e.g., two ideas from this volume each week), and pray that God will help you to achieve it. You will find the index at the back of this volume especially helpful in finding faith-connecting activities relative to specific topics.

• If the ideas in the Concordia Curriculum Guide series seem overwhelming, begin by concentrating on only one subject per month. Or attempt to use the suggested ideas in only two to four subjects the first year. Add two to four subjects per year after that.

Probably the most effective teaching occurs when teachers take advantage of natural opportunities that arise to integrate the faith into their teaching. In those situations, you will often use your own ideas instead of preparing a lesson plan based on teaching suggestions in this guide. Use the white space on the pages of this book to record your own ideas and activities for integrating the Christian faith. We hope this volume will be an incentive to you to create your own effective ways to integrate the Christian faith into the entire school day.

We believe that Christian schools are essential because we believe that our relationship with Jesus Christ permeates every part of our lives. That is why our Christian faith permeates our teaching. That is why we teach in a Christian school.

CHAPTER 1

Vocations in Science and Education

By

Nathan Jastram

Dr. Nathan Jastram was born and raised in Japan, the son of missionary parents. He received a bachelor's degree in classical languages at the University of South Dakota in Vermillion. He earned his master's degree in theology at Concordia Theological Seminary in Fort Wayne, Indiana. He then went on to obtain his doctorate in ancient Near Eastern languages and civilizations—with a dissertation on the Dead Sea Scrolls—from Harvard University (Cambridge, Massachusetts). He taught at Concordia University, River Forest, Illinois, from 1990 to 1999. Dr. Jastram has been teaching at Concordia University Wisconsin, Mequon, since 1999. He is currently the chairman of the theology division.

The Vocation of Scientist

Christian educators live out their vocation as they help others by word, attitude, and example to grow in knowledge, understanding, and skills while sharing with them the love of Jesus. Christians in the field of science serve God and others through their efforts to better understand and apply their understandings of God's creation. Although God has not specifically ordained the vocation of scientist in the Bible, the vocation of science is filled by people who love knowledge and search for wisdom, two attributes often praised in the Bible. Solomon urges, "Get wisdom, get understanding" (Proverbs 4:5 NIV), and rhapsodizes, "How much better to get wisdom than gold, to choose understanding rather than silver!" (Proverbs 16:16 NIV). The wisdom that is extolled so highly begins with the fear of the Lord: "The fear of the LORD is the beginning of wisdom" (Proverbs 9:10 NIV). It continues with the intricacies of creation: "By wisdom the LORD laid the earth's foundations, by understanding He set the heavens in place; by His knowledge the deeps were divided, and the clouds let drop the dew" (Proverbs 3:19–20 NIV). Before the fall into sin, Adam exercised his godly wisdom by engaging in the scientific activity of naming animals (Genesis 2:19–20). Unlike those in the generations to follow him, Adam's understanding came directly from God; no human instruction was available or required.

Discovering How the World Works

When Adam fell into sin, his relationships with Eve, God, and the Earth became marked by disharmony, misunderstanding, and adversity. In some mysterious way, the Earth itself was affected. "Cursed is the ground because of you" (Genesis 3:17 NIV). The apostle Paul writes, "The creation was subjected to frustration, not by its own choice, but by the will of the one who subjected it, in hope that the creation itself will be liberated from its bondage to decay and brought into the glorious freedom of the children of God. We know that the whole creation has been groaning as in the pains of childbirth right up to the present time" (Romans 8:20–22 NIV).

The vocations of Christians who are scientists and of Christian educators are callings through which God shares understanding of the world. Scientists study God's creation to learn more about it. In recent times, it has become possible for scientists to work with the code of life itself as they experiment with DNA. This is a heady development that allows scientists to participate in the creative activity of God, the author and designer of life. Christian educators help students both to understand the world and to find the purpose and significance of their life in the light of God's Word. They assist students as they grow and develop so they may know and appreciate the great value and worth of human life—their own and that of others—as uniquely designed by God and individually redeemed through Christ's life, death, and resurrection.

Demonstrating Love for God and Others

As Christian teachers teach about the created world and as scientists who are Christians work to extend human capabilities and quality of life, they do so with respect for all life and especially for human life. God took special care in creating Adam; He said, "Let Us make man in Our image, in Our likeness, and let them rule over the fish of the sea and the birds of the air, over the livestock, over all the earth, and over all the creatures that move along the ground. So God created man in His own image, in the image of God He created him; male and female He created them" (Genesis 1:26–27 NIV).

Fulfilling their calling, scientists who are Christians demonstrate their love for God and others. Scientists working in the field of medicine, for example, fight against disease so as to lessen its potency, completely eliminate it, or prevent it from happening in the first place. When scientists take on disease, they battle one of the effects of sin that entered the world after the fall.

Christian educators serve God as they assist in the process of human growth and development. They nurture, encourage, and help to mold young lives, celebrating each as God's gift, the object of His creative energy, and the holder of the potential He provides. Christian educators support and nurture each life through instruction rooted in God's Word and as they lift each student up in prayer.

The vocation of Christian educator includes the obligation to value, honor, and serve those God has given them to teach. Properly fulfilled, the vocation of Christian teacher relies on the strength and direction of the Redeemer to work against sin, death, and Satan's power. Christian teachers teach all subjects so as to point students to the enlightening influence of the Savior and the free and rewarding new life He promises. Jesus said, "I am the light of the world. Whoever follows Me will never walk in darkness, but will have the light of life" (John 8:12 NIV).

Between Heaven and Earth

It is the mixture of the earthly and heavenly in human beings that sets them up for great successes and failures. Adam was created as a heavenly creature, in the image and likeness of God, but he was also an earthly creature, distinct from God. Adam's first great temptation was to deny his earthly limitations and grasp at becoming like God with respect to being the ultimate authority to determine what is good and evil. Humans are created to occupy a position between heaven and Earth, and the mixture between the earthly and the heavenly in us is the battlefield on which God and Satan fight. Satan constantly urges people to cast off the shackles of their earthly limitations and enjoy the unfettered prerogatives of their heavenly status. God, on the other hand, commands people to obey Him and to do all they do as His representatives, who, though earthbound, are already citizens of heaven (Philippians 3:20).

The offices of scientist and Christian educator are powerful and full of potential for good or evil. They are so powerful that the specter of these offices gone bad haunts the theologian. Those occupying positions in these offices who make themselves gods, caring nothing about the one true God or His laws of right and wrong, are devils incarnate. They have great power but refuse to acknowledge God's laws governing its use. At best, they are restrained from grievous evil only by their own sense of right and wrong. The scientist misuses his or her vocation when he or she refuses to acknowledge God's primacy, His created orders, or His revealed will. The Christian educator shuts out God when he or she teaches religion yet refuses to let our Savior and His love dominate his or her classroom, lessons, and relationships.

Humans were not created in the image of dogs or trees, but in the image of God. People participate with God in ruling over the world, creating new life, preserving life, and so on. God is the one who "heals all [our] disease" (Psalm 103:3), yet He often does so through human physicians and through drugs that scientists have discovered or invented.

There is simply no theological warrant for the comment attributed to skeptics of a previous era: "If God had wanted people to fly, He would have created them with wings." One might as well say, "If God had wanted people to eat, He would have created them with attached food dispensers" or "If God had wanted people to speak English, He would have created them with an innate knowledge of English." Such silliness assumes that anything that is God's will is always accomplished without any effort on the part of people. On the contrary, it is God's will that we rule over the world, and the hard work that goes into inventing efficient transportation, such as flying, is one aspect of accomplishing that will of God.

Scientists misuse their vocation if they do not participate with God in the work they have been called to do. Since the fall into sin, this work includes efforts to ameliorate the effects of sin, such as healing diseases, increasing fertility (both of the ground and people), and reducing pain. Scientific discoveries and inventions that aid in such work are blessings that God gives us through scientists.

Christian educators misuse their vocation when they fail to properly value, encourage, and delight in each student in their classroom. Contaminated by sin, teaching and learning have never been easy. Still, by God's grace, each new lesson can be as fresh, invigorating, and rewarding as the creative energy God gives the instructor and the knowledge embraced by enlightened young minds. Christian educators are entrusted with great treasures: children received from the creative hand of God, the wisdom of the ages handed down for us to share with them, and understandings established and rooted in God's Word.

In Search of the Path between Heaven and Earth

The scientist and the educator struggle to follow the path to which they have been called, a path between heaven and Earth. It is a struggle with twin dangers: that of flying too high or of not flying at all. In his *Metamorphoses*, Ovid immortalized this struggle through his retelling of the ancient Greek myth of Daedalus and Icarus:

Meanwhile Daedalus, tired of Crete and of his long absence from home, was filled with longing for his own country, but he was shut in by the sea. Then he said: "The king may block my way by land or across the ocean, but the sky, surely, is open, and that is how we shall go. Minos may possess all the rest, but he does not possess the air." With these words, he set his mind to sciences never explored before, and altered the laws of nature. . . . [He built wings of feathers and string and wax and was able to raise himself into the air.] Then he prepared his son to fly too. "I warn you, Icarus," he said, "you must follow a course midway between earth and heaven, in case the sun should scorch your feathers, if you go too high, or the water make them heavy if you are too low. . . . Take me as your guide, and follow me!" . . . [As they began their flight together, a fisherman] caught sight of them as they flew past and stood stock still in astonishment, believing that these creatures who could fly through the air must be gods. . . . [Part way through the journey,] Icarus began to enjoy the thrill of swooping boldly through the air. Drawn on by his eagerness for the open sky, he left his guide and soared upwards, till he came too close to the blazing sun, and it softened the sweet-smelling wax that bound his wings together. The wax melted. Icarus moved his bare arms up and down, but without their feathers they had no purchase on the air. . . . [When Icarus fell into the ocean,] the unhappy father, a father no longer, cried out: "Icarus!" . . . As he was still calling "Icarus" he saw the feather on

the water, and cursed his inventive skill.
(trans. Mary M. Innes [Penguin, 1955])

Generally, the myth of Daedalus and Icarus is used as a cautionary tale against setting one's eyes too high, against altering the laws of nature, and against becoming too much like the gods. After all, the high-flying Icarus dies, and Daedalus "cursed his inventive skill." But the myth loses its potency if it does not also encourage lifting one's eyes up from the ground. There are times when people must fly to escape death or a fate similar to death. Daedalus and Icarus escaped their prison because they flew between heaven and earth with the permission and aid of the gods. Even Icarus would have been saved if he had followed Daedalus's advice: "You must follow a course midway between earth and heaven, in case the sun should scorch your feathers, if you go too high, or the water make them too heavy if you are too low."

What the Greek myth teaches about human beings striving to follow the path between heaven and Earth reminds us of what the Bible teaches. This is the honor and challenge of being a human being. Humans were created in the image and likeness of God and are called to various offices through which God performs His work. People who understand who they are and what they are to do realize that they are sojourners on the earth with an inheritance in heaven and that they are called to follow a path that looks beyond Earth to heaven.

Christian teachers look up from the ground when they respect their students as those for whom our Savior lived, died, and rose again and as they acknowledge and encourage them in their God-given potential to serve in a rewarding and fulfilling vocation. They also look up from the ground when they teach in ways that open vistas of dis-covery for students and challenge students to reach for the highest goals they can acquire in the lives God has given them to live. Making connections between heaven and Earth is essential as Christian educators integrate the faith into science and every other subject taught in a Lutheran school.

Scientists look up from the ground when they follow their calling not only with the aim of discovering the wonders of creation but also with the aim of participating with God in His creative and preserving activity, especially as it relates to exercising God-pleasing rule over the world and relieving the suffering brought into the world through sin. Because nature is not God but has been corrupted by the fall into sin, scientists do not misuse their office when they search for positive ways to change nature. Going mentally from what is earthly to what is heavenly is a natural exercise for those who are in a godly vocation, for those who have been called by God to perform His work.

Christians serving in both science and teaching vocations are encouraged to follow their calling to represent God faithfully, to work for the good of His creation, to do what pleases God, and to function as God's hands. Those who understand who they are and what they are to do realize that God is at the center of the universe, not themselves. They join in the praise of God raised by His people: "You alone are the LORD. You made the heavens, even the highest heavens, and all their starry host, the earth and all that is on it, the seas and all that is in them. You give life to everything, and the multitudes of heaven worship You" (Nehemiah 9:6 NIV).

Chapter 1 adapted from "Scientists Called to Be Like God" by Nathan Jastram, found in *Reading God's World: The Scientific Vocation*, ed. Angus J. L. Menuge (CPH, 2004).

CHAPTER 2

Teaching and Learning Science from a Christian Perspective

Why Integrate Religion with Science?

Knowledge of science helps students understand what makes things happen as they do in the world. The relationships that exist were established by God at the time of creation. The laws of science are human descriptions of these relationships. They are as accurate as our understanding of nature is at the moment, but they are never absolute. These laws are continually refined, expanded, and sometimes abandoned as we uncover additional information about natural phenomenon.

Those teaching in Christian classrooms have the opportunity to point their students to evidence in creation of God's love, wisdom, power, and majesty. Connections made between the concepts of science and the Word of God will help students respond with love, gratitude, awe, and reverence toward their Creator. By the power of the Holy Spirit, science instruction can help students develop these gifts:

Knowledge and understanding

- Learners will appreciate God's power and majesty in establishing and governing the universe and controlling and governing the forces of nature.

- Learners will recognize the constancy and order God designed for the natural world.

- Learners will respond to God's grace by helping make the world a richer, safer, more beautiful place for present and future generations.

Skills

- Learners will use their scientific insights in a life of praise and devotion to God.

- Learners will grow in the ability to think critically and wisely, ever looking to God for guidance when human inquiry fails to find answers or when it leads them away from God's revelation in His Word.

Connecting Science and the Christian Faith

Through the study of science, we learn more about our God—the one who made the world, redeemed it, and supports and preserves all things for the benefit of humanity. Teaching science from a distinctively Christian perspective involves building all lessons on the foundation of God's Word. The message of God's Word relates to science concepts in the following ways.

God made the world: He upholds the universe.

God created all things. He made the universe and everything in it in six days.

He made the world of intricate design and complex order.

God made the plants and animals, each after its own kind. On the sixth day, He created the first people, Adam and Eve, in His image.

The natural world reveals to us the existence of God the Creator (Romans 1:20).

The universe has fallen under the influence of sin.

Yielding to the temptation to abandon God's will, Adam and Eve sinned.

All of creation suffered sin's devastating consequences.

Strife between God and fallen humanity, among people, between people and animals, among animals, and between people and their environment continues as a result of sin (Genesis 3).

We have hope and salvation in Jesus Christ.

God sent Jesus to redeem fallen humanity. Jesus is the Son of God and also a man, born of the Virgin Mary (Galatians 4:4).

As God who created all things, Jesus exerts control over the forces of nature. For example, He stilled the storm (Luke 8:22–25), and He reversed the natural decaying process when He raised Lazarus from the dead (John 11:38–44).

Taking our sin and punishment upon Himself, Jesus overcame even His own death, rising from the dead on Easter morning (Matthew 28:6–7). Through His life, death, and resurrection, Jesus earned forgiveness for all our sin and provides us with a new and eternal life in His name (2 Corinthians 5:17).

By faith God makes us new people in Jesus.

God the Holy Spirit brought us to faith through God's Word.

By faith we understand that the world was formed at God's command (Hebrews 11:3).

God's faithful people respond to the Gospel of Jesus Christ as the Holy Spirit works through God's Word (1 Thessalonians 2:13).

By the working of the Holy Spirit through God's Word, we honor God in these ways:

- We place a high value on all human life.
  - We regard each person as a unique creation of God with distinct characteristics, talents, and abilities.
  - We recognize that Jesus has redeemed all people, including those conceived but not yet born, persons with handicaps, and those unable to care for themselves.
  - We share that God desires all people to receive the gift of salvation He offers freely through Christ Jesus, our Lord.

- We appreciate, care, and manage plants, animals, natural resources, and the environment. Though contaminated by sin, creation still reflects the awesome design and majesty of the Creator. God enables us to use the natural laws and principles He placed into effect to serve and benefit all people by demonstrating good stewardship of all God has given us.
- We use our creativity, abilities, skills, and technology to glorify God and serve others.
  - We recognize scientific knowledge, understanding, and insights as God's good gifts to His people.
  - We thank and praise Him for all He has given to us.
  - We use technological advancements to share the love of Christ—especially the Good News of Jesus—with all others.

Best Practices for Science Education in Christian Schools

Teachers in Christian classrooms have been given the opportunity to teach science in a context that integrates their faith in Jesus Christ and the forgiveness and new life that are theirs in Him. This curriculum guide integrates the Christian faith into science education based on the following principles.

Students learn science concepts most effectively when they explore concrete examples. We serve students best by providing them with hands-on activities that are pertinent to the concerns of their daily lives.

In a world that is growing increasingly dependent on the contributions of science, scientific literacy is an important educational goal for all students. Teachers help students achieve scientific literacy by recognizing and responding to the needs of individual students and to the cultural diversity of students.

Science education is enhanced when based upon reliable educational standards that guide student attainment, curriculum content, and teaching practices. These include the Benchmarks of Science Literacy prepared by Project 2061, a long-term educational reform project of the American Association for the Advancement of Science, and the National Science Educational Standards prepared by the National Research Council.

Students in our nation's schools learn science with an emphasis on the big ideas or common themes of science as identified by Project 2061. Four common themes are systems, models, constancy and change, and scale.

When Faith and Science Seem in Conflict

Science is the search for new knowledge and understandings about creation and how it functions. This searching involves investigation, observation, and the formulation of hypotheses and conclusions. Students in Lutheran schools need to be encouraged to reason, think creatively, and project outcomes. These abilities are God's gifts, and God is honored when these gifts are received with thanksgiving and used to serve Him and others.

When faith and scientific theories seem in conflict, those teaching in Lutheran schools do well to provide students with special guidance. Consider, for example, the creation/evolution controversy. Christian teachers should not avoid this issue. Instead, teachers need to help students face unbiblical perspectives as one important dimension of the education they provide. Opposition to the words of Scripture is not new and can be expected by those who profess faith in Christ Jesus. Part of growing and maturing as a child of God involves learning to respond to critics, skeptics, and opponents to the teachings of God's Word with gentleness and respect (1 Peter 3:15), confident in God's love and grace, and secure in the knowledge God has given us through His holy Word.

Much of the scientific community rallies behind evolutionary philosophy with a zeal many regard as religious in nature. Followers of the theory of evolution cannot rightfully be cast as ill-informed or easily duped. Most have received their education in an environment that has regarded evolution as an axiom not to be questioned. Those teaching in Lutheran schools can help their students respond to concepts of evolution—and those who support the evolutionary belief system—using approaches that are honest, realistic, and appropriate.

The following considerations may be helpful when issues such as evolution surface in lessons and discussions.

God is the Creator. God's Word says, "By Him all things were created, in heaven and on earth, visible and invisible" (Colossians 1:16). As the Holy Spirit works through the means of grace, followers of Jesus believe what God says about creation even though they were not there to see it. This belief is founded upon faith. "Faith is the assurance of things hoped for, the conviction of things not seen" (Hebrews 11:1). "By faith we understand that the universe was created by the word of God, so that what is seen was not made out of things that are visible" (Hebrews 11:3). In Genesis 1 and 2, God tells us that He created the world in six days. Although many details are omitted from the account, we do know that God made everything with a specific plan and purpose in mind and that human beings are the crown of His creation.

God gave people curiosity; therefore, questioning the intricacies of God's creation so that we may better serve God and others is not wrong. As long as scientists regard theories as theories and are willing to recognize the limitations of science, God's people are, and can continue to be, served well by the unfolding advancements in our understanding about the world God has made for us to enjoy.

Evolutionary theory offers a partial explanation about the origins of life. It does not, however, answer all questions about when, where, and why life ultimately began. After decades of research and study, many holes in the theory remain. The current debate over the appropriateness of including intelligent design as part of the science curriculum in public schools suggests one big unanswered question in the evolutionary mode: what is the source of all life?

Science and faith are two of the many blessings God has given us. People come to know and believe in Jesus Christ as their Savior by faith as a result of the work of the Holy Spirit through the means of grace, not through the workings of science. Through science and scientific inquiry, we learn about creation—the world God made and the laws under which it operates.

The words of a Lutheran educator from a previous decade wisely remind us, "In short, the teacher owes it to his pupils to deal with the creation-evolution problem. Before doing so, however, he must acquaint himself with the theological and scientific factors involved. Only then will he begin to measure up to the teaching task—a task which calls for encouraging faith to take over where reason falters, for letting the creator remain creator, and for listening with full but critical ear to what the scientist would tell."

Science and Faith Activities, Insights, and Discussion Suggestions Provided in This Volume

Included in chapter 5 of this volume, following each standard, you will find activities, insights, and discussion suggestions for helping young people relate science concepts to themselves as children of God through faith in Christ Jesus. These learning activities help students focus on important principles of science in the context of God's providence and grace.

Care has been taken to make connections that

• uphold God's Word as truth and science as the search for truth;

• are natural and relevant;

• stimulate a discussion of Christian values and applications for the new life we have through Christ Jesus;

• prepare and equip students for times when they will be forced to react to popular belief systems that contradict the Word of God.

CHAPTER 3

Using the Benchmarks for Science Literacy

In 1993, the American Association for the Advancement of Science (AAAS), specifically Project 2061's Science for All Americans (SFAA), published a list of Benchmarks for Science Literacy. This resource was developed by teachers and administrators with the help and input of education specialists and scientists. Its intent is to provide a curriculum design tool helpful to those planning curriculum so that desired science literacy outcomes can be obtained. These benchmarks are organized by grade level according to the following categories.

The Scientific Worldview

Kindergarten–Grade 2

Grades 3–5

Grades 6–8

Grades 9–12

Scientific Inquiry

Kindergarten–Grade 2

Grades 3–5

Grades 6–8

Grades 9–12

The Scientific Enterprise

Kindergarten–Grade 2

Grades 3–5

Grades 6–8

Grades 9–12

These benchmarks have been adapted as follows to incorporate elements of the Christian faith.

A. The Scientific Worldview

Kindergarten–Grade 2

By the end of the second grade, students should know this:

- When a science investigation is done the way it was done before, they can expect to get a very similar result because of the laws God put into place at creation.

- Science investigations generally work the same way in different places.

Grades 3–5

By the end of the fifth grade, students should know this:

- Results of similar scientific investigations seldom turn out exactly the same. Sometimes this is because of unexpected differences in the things being investigated, sometimes because of unrealized differences in the methods used or in the circumstances in which the investigation is carried out, and sometimes just because of uncertainties in observations. It is not always easy to tell which. Some of these differences characterize life in our fallen world as contrasted with the perfection our first parents enjoyed in Eden.

Grades 6–8

By the end of the eighth grade, students should know this:

- When similar investigations give different results, the scientific challenge is to judge whether the differences are trivial or significant, and it often takes further studies to decide. Even with similar results, scientists may wait until an investigation has been repeated many times before accepting the results as correct.

- Scientific knowledge is subject to modification as new information challenges prevailing theories and as a new theory leads to looking at old observations in a new way. Science modifies and originates theories to answer questions about the world God created.

- Some scientific knowledge is very old and yet is still applicable today.

- Some matters cannot be examined usefully in a scientific way. Among them are matters that by their nature cannot be tested objectively and those that are essentially matters of morality. Science can sometimes be used to inform ethical decisions by identifying the likely consequences of particular actions but cannot be used to establish that some action is either moral or immoral. "How" questions can be answered using the scientific method. "Why" questions are often those best explored and answered as matters of faith as guided by the Holy Spirit through the Word of God.

Grades 9–12

By the end of the twelfth grade,
students should know this:

- Scientists assume that the universe is a vast single system in which the basic rules are the same everywhere. The rules may range from very simple to extremely complex, but scientists operate on the belief that the rules can be discovered by careful, systematic study. Their findings help us to better understand creation.

- From time to time, major shifts occur in the scientific view of how the world works. More often, however, the changes that take place in the body of scientific knowledge are small modifications of prior knowledge. Change and continuity are persistent features of science.

- No matter how well one theory fits observations, a new theory might fit them just as well or better or might fit a wider range of observations. In science, the testing, revising, and occasional discarding of theories, new and old, never ends. This ongoing process leads to an increasingly better understanding of how

things work in the world, but not to absolute truth. Evidence for the value of this approach is given by the improving ability of scientists to offer reliable explanations and make accurate predictions. God's Word, however, provides absolute truth. Jesus, the author and perfecter of our faith, referred to Himself as the ultimate truth. He said, "I am the way, and the truth, and the life. No one comes to the Father except through Me" (John 14:6).

B. Scientific Inquiry

Kindergarten–Grade 2

By the end of the second grade,
students should know this:

- People can often learn about things around them by just observing those things carefully, but sometimes they can learn more by doing something to the things and noting what happens.

- Tools such as thermometers, magnifiers, rulers, or balances often give more information about things than can be obtained by just observing things without their help.

- Describing things as accurately as possible is important in science because it enables people to compare their observations with those of others.

- When people give different descriptions of the same thing, it is usually a good idea to make some fresh observations instead of just arguing about who is right. Such differences are certain to occur from time to time because we live in a fallen world.

Grades 3–5

By the end of the fifth grade,
students should know this:

- Scientific investigations may take many different forms, including observing what things are like or what is happening somewhere, collecting specimens for analysis, and doing experiments. Investigations can focus on physical, biological, and social questions.

- Results of scientific investigations are seldom exactly the same, but if the differences are large, it is important to try to figure out why. One reason for following directions carefully and for keeping records of one's work is to provide information on what might have caused the differences.

- Scientists' explanations about what happens in the world come partly from what they observe, partly from what they think. Sometimes scientists have different explanations for the same set of observations. That usually leads to their making more observations to resolve the differences.

- Scientists do not pay much attention to claims about how something they know about works unless the claims are backed up with evidence that can be confirmed and with a logical argument. Advancements in knowledge and understanding are among God's gifts and evidence of His love and grace for all people.

Grades 6–8

By the end of the eighth grade, students should know this:

- Scientists differ greatly in what phenomena they study and how they go about their work. Although there is no fixed set of steps that all scientists follow, scientific investigations usually involve the collection of relevant evidence, the use of logical reasoning, and the application of imagination in devising hypotheses and explanations to make sense of the collected evidence.

- If more than one variable changes at the same time in an experiment, the outcome of the experiment may not be clearly attributable to any one of the variables. It may not always be possible to prevent outside variables from influencing the outcome of an investigation (or even to identify all of the variables), but collaboration among investigators can often lead to research designs that are able to deal with such situations.

- What people expect to observe often affects what they actually do observe. Strong beliefs

about what should happen in particular circumstances can prevent people from detecting other results. Scientists know about this danger to objectivity and take steps to try and avoid it when designing investigations and examining data. One safeguard is to have different investigators conduct independent studies of the same questions. Imperfect studies and inappropriate applications of studies characterize life in our sin-contaminated world.

- New ideas in science sometimes spring from unexpected findings, and they usually lead to new investigations.

Grades 9–12

By the end of the twelfth grade, students should know this:

- Investigations are conducted for different reasons, including to explore new phenomena, to check on previous results, to test how well a theory predicts, and to compare different theories.

- Hypotheses are widely used in science for choosing what data to pay attention to and what additional data to seek, and for guiding the interpretation of the data (both new and previously available).

- Sometimes, scientists can control conditions in order to obtain evidence. When that is not possible for practical or ethical reasons, they try to observe as wide a range of natural occurrences as possible to be able to discern patterns.

- There are different traditions in science about what is investigated and how, but they all have in common certain basic beliefs about the value of evidence, logic, and good arguments. There is agreement that progress in all fields of science depends on intelligence, hard work, imagination, and even chance.

- Scientists in any one research group tend to see things alike, so even groups of scientists may have trouble being entirely objective about their methods and findings. For that reason, scientific teams are expected to seek out the possible sources of bias in the design of their investigations and in their data analysis. Checking each other's results and explanations helps, but that is no guarantee against bias.

- In the short run, new ideas that do not mesh well with mainstream ideas in science often encounter vigorous criticism. In the long run, theories are judged by how they fit with other theories, the range of observations they explain, how well they explain observations, and how effective they are in predicting new findings.

- New ideas in science are limited by the context in which they are conceived, are often rejected by the scientific establishment, sometimes spring from unexpected findings, and usually grow slowly through contributions from many investigators. By God's grace, new ideas help, benefit, and enlighten those affected by them.

C. The Scientific Enterprise

Kindergarten–Grade 2

By the end of the 2nd grade,
students should know this:

- Everybody can do science and invent things and ideas.

- In doing science, it is often helpful to work with a team and to share findings with others. All team members should reach their own individual conclusions, however, about what the findings mean.

- A lot can be learned about plants and animals by observing them closely, but care must be taken to know the needs of living things and how to provide for them in the classroom. Properly caring for plants and animals is one of the ways people share God's love in the world around them.

Grades 3–5

By the end of the fifth grade,
students should know this:

- Science is an adventure that people everywhere can take part in, as they have for many centuries.

- Clear communication is an essential part of doing science. It enables scientists to inform others about their work, expose their ideas to criticism by other scientists, and stay informed about scientific discoveries around the world.

- Doing science involves many different kinds of work and engages men and women of all ages and backgrounds, providing Christians involved in science many opportunities to share the Good News of salvation by grace through faith in Jesus.

Grades 6–8

By the end of the eighth grade,
students should know this:

- Important contributions to the advancement of science, mathematics, and technology have been made by different kinds of people, in different cultures, at different times. Until recently, women and racial minorities, because of restrictions on their education and employment opportunities, were essentially left out of much of the formal work of the science establishment. The remarkable few who overcame those obstacles were even then likely to have their work disregarded by the science establishment. These behaviors disregard God's will as explained in God's Word. Jesus died to redeem and save all people.

- No matter who does science and mathematics or invents things, or when or where they do it, the knowledge and technology that result can eventually become available to everyone in the world as a great blessing from God.

- Scientists are employed by colleges and universities, business and industry, hospitals, and many government agencies. Their places of work include offices, classrooms, laboratories, farms, factories, and natural field settings ranging from the ocean floor to outer space.

- In research involving human subjects, the ethics of science require that potential subjects be fully informed about the risks and benefits associated with the research and of their right to refuse to participate. Science ethics also demand that scientists must not knowingly subject co-workers, students, the neighborhood, or the community to health or property risks without their prior knowledge and consent. Because animals cannot make informed choices, special care must be taken in using them in scientific research.

- Computers have become invaluable in science because they speed up and extend people's ability to collect, store, compile, and analyze data; prepare research reports; and share data and ideas with investigators all over the world.

- Accurate record-keeping, openness, and replication are essential for maintaining an investigator's credibility with other scientists and society.

Grades 9–12

By the end of the twelfth grade, students should know this:

- The early Egyptian, Greek, Chinese, Hindu, and Arabic cultures are responsible for many scientific and mathematical ideas and technological inventions.

- Modern science is based on traditions of thought that came together in Europe about five hundred years ago. People from all cultures now contribute to that tradition.

- History often depends on scientific and technological developments; progress in science and invention depends heavily on what else is happening in society.

- Science disciplines differ from one another in what is studied, the techniques used, and the outcomes sought, but they share a common purpose and philosophy, and all are part of the same scientific enterprise. Although each discipline provides a conceptual structure for organizing and pursuing knowledge, many problems are studied by scientists using information and skills from many disciplines. Disciplines do not have fixed boundaries, and it often happens that new scientific disciplines are being formed where existing ones meet and that some subdisciplines spin off to become new disciplines in their own right.

- Current ethics in science hold that research involving human subjects may be conducted only with the informed consent of the subjects, even if this constraint limits some kinds of potentially important research or influences the results. When it comes to participation in research that could pose risks to society, most scientists believe that a decision to participate or not is a matter of personal ethics rather than professional ethics.

- Scientists can bring information, insights, and analytical skills to bear on matters of public concern. Acting in their areas of expertise, scientists can help people understand the likely causes of events and estimate their possible effects. Outside their areas of expertise, however, scientists should enjoy no special credibility. Where their own personal, institutional, or community interests are at stake, scientists as a group can be expected to be no less biased than other groups are about their perceived interests.

- The strongly held traditions of science, including its commitment to peer review and publication, serve to keep the vast majority of scientists well within the bounds of ethical professional behavior. Deliberate deceit is rare and likely to be exposed sooner or later by the scientific enterprise itself. When violations of these scientific ethical traditions are discovered, they are strongly condemned by the scientific community, and the violators then have difficulty regaining the respect of other scientists. Like all of us, scientists are accountable to their Creator and have been forgiven by Him through the merits of Christ Jesus, our Lord.

- Funding influences the direction of science by virtue of the decisions that are made on which research to support. Research funding comes from various federal government agencies, industry, and private foundations.

Chapter 3 adapted from materials by the American Association for the Advancement of Science (1993).

19

CHAPTER 4

Science Curriculum Standards for Students in Grade 8

This chapter includes science standards that have been compiled from the individual state departments of education. They are organized, grade by grade, into the following four areas:

1. Physical Sciences

2. Life Sciences

3. Natural Sciences

4. Scientific Processes and Approaches

The Concordia standards have been systematized according to the following numerical designations to indicate grade level, area, category, and performance objective:

- The first digit indicates the grade level (e.g., the *2* in *2.3.1.8* designates that the performance expectation is for grade 2).

- The second digit indicates the area of science (as listed above) addressed by the standard (e.g., the *3* in *2.3.1.8* designates the standard as a natural sciences area since *3* is the number for natural sciences.

- The third digit indicates a category within the area. These categories are the same at every grade level (e.g., the *1* in *2.3.1.8* relates to the category of space studies, which is the first category of natural sciences at every grade level).

- The fourth digit indicates the number of the specific performance expectation. These expectations will vary from level to level (e.g., the *8* in *2.3.1.8* is found in the natural sciences area of the grade 2 standards relating to the category of space studies, refers to the eighth item in that category).

Chapter 5 provides faith-integration activities organized by category. These activities provide many opportunities to teach aspects of the Christian faith in conjunction with each area of the science curriculum. Each activity is keyed to a specific performance expectation.

A complete list of science standards performance expectations for this grade level is provided on the remaining pages of this chapter. In order to offer a well-coordinated curriculum design, the science education objectives for each grade level are related to and connected with the standards provided at other grade levels. Teachers and schools are invited to use the CD that is included in the *Concordia Curriculum Guide: Science* volume at each grade level to modify the Concordia science education standards for use in their own particular situation.

PHYSICAL SCIENCES

8.1   **Eighth-grade students in Lutheran schools will understand concepts related to the physical sciences.**

8.1.1   **Composition of Matter**

8.1.1.1   Construct a classification system based on similarities and differences.

8.1.1.2   Explain that all matter is composed of atoms.

8.1.1.3   Illustrate the structure of the atom, including identifying and explaining the activities of protons, neutrons, and electrons.

8.1.1.4   Describe the basic structure of matter by identifying the elements and researching their distinct properties and atomic structures.

8.1.1.5   Define compounds.

8.1.1.6   Give examples of several compounds, and describe their properties.

8.1.1.7   Identify molecules as the smallest part of a compound.

8.1.1.8   Compare the properties of compounds with the properties of the elements from which they are made.

8.1.1.9   Demonstrate physical processes, include freezing and boiling, in which materials change form but where there is no chemical reaction.

8.1.1.10   Explain that although mixtures can be separated using physical properties, compounds cannot be separated using physical properties.

8.1.1.11   Affirm chemical reactions as processes in which atoms are rearranged into different combinations of molecules.

8.1.1.12   Use atoms to explain the conservation of matter, especially in chemical reactions.

8.1.1.13   Illustrate that chemical reactions usually liberate heat or absorb it.

8.1.1.14   Describe a chemical reaction, naming the reactants and products when given a symbolic equation, a word equation, or a description of the reaction.

8.1.1.15   Determine whether a solution is acidic, basic, or neutral.

8.1.1.16   Explain that the organization of the periodic table is based on the properties of the elements and reflects the structure of atoms.

8.1.1.17   Identify regions on the periodic table that correspond to metals, nonmetals, and noble gases.

8.1.1.18   Explain that each element has a specific number of protons in the nucleus (the atomic number) and each isotope of the element has a different but specific number of neutrons in the nucleus.

8.1.1.19   Give the number of protons and electrons in a neutral atom based on the atom's atomic number.

8.1.1.20   Identify the mass number of an atom as the sum of the protons and neutrons in the atom.

8.1.1.21   Differentiate the arrangement and motion of atoms or molecules of solids, liquids, and gases.

8.1.1.22   Define molecules as groups of atoms that are chemically combined.

8.1.1.23   Give the location, relative charge, and relative mass of protons, neutrons, and electrons.

8.1.1.24   Classify substances by their properties, using data regarding melting temperature, density, hardness, and thermal and electrical conductivity.

8.1.1.25   Define density as mass per unit volume.

8.1.1.26   Calculate the density of substances (regular and irregular solids and liquids) from measurements of mass and volume.

8.1.1.27   Demonstrate that the buoyant force on an object in a fluid is an upward force equal to the weight of the fluid the object has displaced.

8.1.1.28   Predict accurately whether an object will float or sink.

8.1.1.29   Explain that the total mass of a system remains the same throughout a chemical reaction because the number of atoms of each element remains the same.

8.1.1.30   Describe atoms and molecules as being constantly in motion, and explain that higher temperature results in increased motion.

8.1.1.31   Explain the principles of chemistry that underlie the functioning of biological systems.

8.1.1.32   Explore the importance of carbon in the chemistry of living things because of its ability to combine with itself and other elements in many ways.

8.1.1.33   Illustrate that living organisms are made of molecules consisting largely of carbon, hydrogen, nitrogen, oxygen, phosphorus, and sulfur.

8.1.1.34   Research living organisms to understand the idea that organisms have many different kinds of molecules, including small ones, such as water and salt, and very large ones, such as carbohydrates, fats, proteins, and DNA.

8.1.2   Magnetism, Force, and Motion

8.1.2.1   Recognize that gravity holds objects such as planets, moon, and satellites in their orbits.

8.1.2.2   Describe the role of electromagnets in electric motors, electric generators, and other common devices.

8.1.3   Energy

8.1.3.1   Use position, time, distance, and speed to describe the motion and distance an object travels.

8.1.3.2   Illustrate the difference between accelerated and constant motions using time, distance, and speed.

8.1.3.3   Use change in speed and time to calculate acceleration.

8.1.3.4   Explain that an object's change of position (motion) is always judged and determined in comparison to a reference point.

8.1.3.5   Acknowledge motion as a change in the position of an object, characterized by a speed and direction, as time changes.

8.1.3.6   Describe how an unbalanced force acting on an object changes that object's speed and/or direction.

8.1.3.7   Show how waves transfer energy.

8.1.3.8   Create vibrations in materials to produce waves that spread away from the source in all directions.

8.1.3.9   Describe conduction and convection based on molecular motion.

8.1.3.10   Acknowledge that radiation does not require matter to transfer heat energy.

8.1.3.11   Identify ways conduction, convection, and radiation can be reduced.

8.1.3.12   Describe different forms of energy (e.g., electrical, mechanical, chemical, thermal, nuclear, radiant, and acoustic).

8.1.3.13   Explain that heating is caused by adding heat energy and that cooling is caused by removing heat energy.

8.1.3.14 Explain that energy derived from renewable resources such as wind and water will be available indefinitely.

8.1.3.15 Construct a simple series circuit and a simple parallel circuit using a battery, wire, and two or more resistors such as lightbulbs or buzzers.

8.1.3.16 Explain that although energy can change forms, the total amount of energy remains constant.

8.1.3.17 Describe energy transformation in a simple closed system (e.g., a flashlight).

8.1.4   Simple Machines

8.1.4.1 Compare the structure and functioning of simple machines with the structure and functioning of the joints of the human body.

8.1.4.2 Explain how simple machines do work when functioning either individually or together with other simple machines.

8.1.5   Sound

8.1.5.1 Explain how sound travels.

8.1.5.2 Characterize sound.

8.1.6   Light

8.1.6.1 Explain reflection, absorption, refraction, and shadows.

8.1.6.2 Recognize the colors in the spectrum.

8.1.6.3 Describe why objects are a certain color.

LIFE SCIENCES

8.2   Eighth-grade students in Lutheran schools will understand concepts related to the life sciences.

8.2.1   Plants and Animals

8.2.1.1   Critique the branching diagrams developed by scientists to classify living organisms that share characteristics.

8.2.1.2   Illustrate the complementary nature of structure and function in the anatomy and physiology of plants and animals.

8.2.1.3   Explain the levels of organization of living things, including cells, tissues, organs, systems, and organisms, and the ways these relate to one another.

8.2.1.4   Explain how photosynthesis and cellular respiration capture and release energy.

8.2.1.5   Describe the function of the nucleus in both plant and animal cells.

8.2.1.6   Explain that green plants use carbon dioxide and water in the presence of sunlight to make food (sugar).

8.2.1.7   Describe how organisms take in nutrients, which they use to provide energy for the work that cells do and to make the building materials they need.

8.2.1.8   Give the structure and function of parts of animal cells, including the cell membrane, cytoplasm, vacuole, nucleus, chromosomes, and mitochondria.

8.2.1.9   Describe the structures and functions of the parts of plant cells, including the cell wall, nucleus, chromosomes, vacuole, cell membrane, chloroplast, cytoplasm, and mitochondria.

8.2.1.10   Explain mitosis and cell differentiation.

8.2.1.11   Describe the levels of organization and structure of organisms in terms of specialized cells, tissues, organs, and organ systems.

8.2.1.12   Explain the functions of individual organs and the effects of the failure of any part of the organ or system.

8.2.1.13   Explain the structures and processes used by flowering plants to produce pollen, ovules, seeds, and fruit.

8.2.1.14   Explain that proteins are building materials and that carbohydrates and fats provide plants and animals with energy.

8.2.1.15   Tell how toxic substances, such as household chemicals, lead, and radon, affect the structure and function of organisms.

8.2.2   Ecosystems

8.2.2.1   Illustrate the interrelatedness of the global food webs, the ocean food web, and the land food web.

8.2.2.2   Tell how matter is transformed between the physical environment and organisms (e.g., tell how nitrogen is cycled through the food web).

8.2.2.3   Explain how the environment can be changed by natural processes, including cyclical climate change, flooding, volcanic eruptions, drought, soil erosion, sedimentation in watersheds, natural selection, population, cycles, extinction, forest fires, and deforestation.

8.2.2.4   Describe how overpopulation affects an ecosystem.

8.2.2.5   Describe how organisms or populations may interact with one another through symbiotic relationships and how some species interact so closely that neither could survive without the other (e.g., predator and prey, parasitism, mutualism, and commensalisms).

8.2.2.6 Tell how both gradual (climactic) and sudden (floods and fires) changes in the environment affect the survival of organisms and populations.

8.2.3   Human Life

8.2.3.1 Explain the functioning of various bodily systems, including the skeletal and reproductive systems in humans, and the effects of various diseases on these systems.

8.2.3.2 Tell how pathogens, such as bacteria, viruses, and fungi, interfere with normal body functions.

8.2.3.3 Explain how parasites, such as tapeworms, interfere with normal body functions.

8.2.3.4 Describe the body's defense system against infectious agents.

8.2.3.5 Tell how human activities produce changes in the natural processes (e.g., through use of energy resources, development, disposal of waste).

8.2.3.6 Identify harmful and helpful health habits and practices.

8.2.4   Heredity

8.2.4.1 Recognize that genes carry genetic information located on chromosomes in cells.

8.2.4.2 Explain the relationship between inherited traits and genes.

8.2.4.3 Explain that in some organisms, genes come from a single parent (yeast, bacteria), while in organisms that have sexes, half the genes come from one parent and half the genes come from the other parent.

8.2.4.4 Distinguish between acquired traits and acquired skills.

8.2.4.5 Explain that asexual reproduction results in the production of organisms that are genetically identical to the parent.

8.2.4.6 Explain that in sexual reproduction new combinations of traits are produced that may increase or decrease an organism's chance for survival.

8.2.4.7 Tell how variations in structure, behavior, or physiology allow some organisms to enhance their reproductive success and survival chances in a given environment.

8.2.4.8 Acknowledge that sexual reproduction produces organisms similar but not genetically identical to either parent.

8.2.4.9 Acknowledge that new varieties of plants and animals have been developed through selective breeding for specific traits.

8.2.5   Life in the Past

8.2.5.1 Describe adaptations that include variations in structures, behaviors, and physiology, such as spiny leaves on a cactus and antibiotic resistance in bacteria.

8.2.5.2 Explain that extinction occurs when the adaptive traits of a population do not support its survival.

8.2.5.3 Connect the theory of evolution to the diversity of species.

8.2.5.4 Describe diversity of species as developed through gradual processes over many generations.

8.2.5.5 Explain that an organism adapted to a particular environment may become extinct if the environment undergoes a change.

8.2.5.6 Explain several factors that cause extinction of species.

NATURAL SCIENCES

8.3 **Eighth-grade students in Lutheran schools will understand concepts related to the natural sciences.**

8.3.1 **Space Studies, eighth-grade students**

8.3.1.1 Identify the universe as consisting of billions of galaxies, which are classified by shape.

8.3.1.2 Affirm that interstellar distances are measured in light-years.

8.3.1.3 Report on the appearance, general composition, relative position and size, and motion of objects in the solar system, including planets, planetary satellites, comets, and asteroids.

8.3.1.4 Explain how the regular and predictable motions of objects in the solar system relate to the phenomena of days, years, seasons, eclipses, tides, and moon cycles.

8.3.1.5 Acknowledge gravitational force as the dominant force determining motions in the solar system and keeping the planets in orbit around the sun.

8.3.1.6 Describe the life cycle of a star.

8.3.1.7 Relate a planet's revolution to the length of its solar year and its distance from the sun.

8.3.1.8 Explain the cause of the phases of the moon.

8.3.1.9 Describe how lunar and solar eclipses occur.

8.3.1.10 Explain the cause of high and low tides.

8.3.1.11 Describe spring tides and neap tides in terms of the position of the moon and sun relative to Earth.

8.3.1.12 Relate the tilt of Earth's axis, Earth's revolution around the sun, and the uneven heating of Earth's surface.

8.3.1.13 Explain how the tilt of Earth's axis and its revolution determine the progression of seasons.

8.3.1.14 Tell why different places on Earth's surface can have a different amount of daylight during any single rotation.

8.3.1.15 Relate the period of daylight at any point on Earth to latitude and the direction of Earth's axis with respect to the sun.

8.3.2 **Land and Water**

8.3.2.1 Explain the Earth's composition, structure, and processes (classification of rocks and minerals, effects of the movement of crustal plates, weathering, erosion, volcanic activity, earthquakes, rock cycle).

8.3.2.2 Explain the interaction of Earth systems and the atmosphere (weather and climate, water cycle, climate change over time, currents).

8.3.2.3 Describe the Earth's crust and interior, explaining that the Earth's crust is divided into tectonic plates riding on top of the slowly moving magma found in the mantle.

8.3.2.4 Recognize tectonic plate motion as the cause of most geological events, including earthquakes, volcanic eruptions, hot spots, and mountain building.

8.3.2.5 Make models to show the size and shape of the Earth, its surface, and its interior.

8.3.2.6 Relate the processes involved in the rock cycle to thermal energy and forces in the mantle that drive tectonic plate motions.

8.3.2.7 Explain the creation of landforms through both destructive (e.g., weathering and erosion) and constructive (e.g., crustal deformation, volcanic activity, and the deposition of sediment) activities.

8.3.2.8 Tell how folding, faulting, and uplifting rearrange the rock layers so that the youngest layer is not always the layer found on top.

8.3.2.9 Identify transform, divergent, and convergent as the three types of plate boundaries and explain how activity along these boundaries cause various landforms such as mountains, volcanoes, and ocean trenches.

8.3.2.10 Explain how convection currents within the mantle drive the movement of Earth's crustal plates and plate boundaries.

8.3.2.11 Tell how igneous, sedimentary, and metamorphic rocks are formed.

8.3.2.12 Describe and explain the rock cycle.

8.3.2.13 Characterize the minerals that make up rocks.

8.3.2.14 Explain the distribution and circulation of water on Earth through glaciers, surface water, ground water, oceans, and atmosphere (water cycle).

8.3.2.15 Compare the physical properties of fresh water and salt water.

8.3.2.16 Describe ways to use the Earth's resources wisely, since they are finite.

8.3.2.17 Relate the impact of available transportation to decreased dependence on local resources.

8.3.2.18 Tell how smoke, smog, and sewage can change the environment negatively depending on the amount and time involved.

8.3.3 Weather and Seasons

8.3.3.1 Explain the functions of the layers of Earth's atmosphere.

8.3.3.2 Relate latitude and climate.

8.3.3.3 Relate temperature and precipitation of an area to the relative location of mountains and the proximity to large bodies of water and to warm and cold ocean currents.

8.3.3.4 Describe the global effects of volcanic eruptions, greenhouse gases, and El Niño.

8.3.3.5 Identify and explain the weather patterns associated with high and low pressure systems and frontal systems.

8.3.3.6 Explain the atmospheric and hydrospheric conditions associated with the formation and development of hurricanes, tornadoes, and thunderstorms.

8.3.3.7 Tell how various tools, such as barometers, thermometers, anemometers, and psychrometers, are used to collect weather data and forecast weather conditions.

SCIENTIFIC PROCESSES AND APPROACHES

8.4   **Eighth-grade students in Lutheran schools will understand concepts related to scientific processes and approaches.**

8.4.1   **Scientific Methods**

8.4.1.1   Conduct investigations that include developing a hypothesis and using appropriate tools and technology to test, collect, and display data.

8.4.1.2   Define and explain sample size and control as they pertain to science investigations.

8.4.1.3   Collect and evaluate for scientific accuracy print and nonprint resources helpful in conducting scientific investigations.

8.4.1.4   Keep accurate records and realize that if more than one variable is changed at a time in an experiment, the results cannot be attributed to any one of the variables.

8.4.1.5   Gather, interpret, and explain data in written and oral forms, using tables, charts, maps, graphs, diagrams, or symbols.

8.4.1.6   Use topographic and geologic maps in conjunction with investigations.

8.4.1.7   Research and present information regarding the history of science, including the contributions to the understanding of matter made by Antoine Lavoisier and Marie and Pierre Curie.

8.4.1.8   Build an object or create a solution to a problem given more than two constraints (e.g., limits of cost and time for design and production, supply of materials, and environmental effects).

8.4.1.9   Analyze the effectiveness of a product design or solution.

8.4.1.10   Use mean, median, and mode to interpret quantitative data.

8.4.1.11   Differentiate between description (e.g., observation and summary) and explanation (e.g., inference, prediction, significance, and importance).

8.4.1.12   Tell why it is important not to let bias affect observations in a scientific investigation.

8.4.1.13   Observe repeated events, occurrences, or cycles to identify and explain patterns and make predictions.

8.4.1.14   Generate directions so that others are able to repeat a procedure.

8.4.1.15   Explain why scientists support claims only when they are backed by observations that can be confirmed.

8.4.1.16   Tell the importance of keeping accurate records of data when conducting scientific investigations.

8.4.1.17   Recognize whether data increases, decreases, or remains unchanged, and formulate conclusions based on data.

8.4.1.18   Identify repeated elements in sequences and symmetries in designs and structures, and speak, write, or draw to repeat a sequence.

8.4.1.19   Use data to support conclusions, plans, or solutions.

8.4.1.20   Evaluate evidence, interpret data, and report on the investigative process and its results in written and oral presentations.

8.4.2   **Applying Scientific Knowledge**

8.4.2.1   Recognize the slope of the linear graph as the constant in the relationship y=kx, and apply this principle in interpreting graphs constructed from data.

8.4.2.2   Apply simple mathematic relationships to determine a missing quantity in a mathematic expression given the two remaining terms (including speed = distance/time, density = mass/volume, force = pressure × area, volume = area × height).

8.4.2.3   Distinguish between linear and nonlinear relationships on a graph of data.

8.4.2.4   Identify criteria for a well-designed investigation, including testing only one variable, using a control, observing and measuring results, completing multiple trials, selecting appropriate materials and equipment, developing clear and logical directions, and following safe procedures.

8.4.2.5   Design an object or system to address a specific problem or issue.

8.4.2.6   Modify a product or design, and assess whether the modification has led to other problems or has improved the product.

8.4.2.7   Explain the advantages and disadvantages of possible decisions about an issue.

8.4.2.8   Tell how scientific information was used to make a decision.

8.4.2.9   Formulate a plan outlining materials necessary, steps needed, and time required.

8.4.2.10   Give two or more possible solutions to a problem, and then support a choice using scientific evidence.

8.4.2.11   Apply logical thinking and careful review of data to theories and scientific models.

8.4.2.12   Explain how men and women of various cultures and backgrounds and people with disabilities have contributed to the advancement of science and technology (e.g., John Dalton, Charles Darwin, Gregor Mendel, Jonas Salk).

8.4.2.13   Identify careers in science, and explain what people must do to prepare for them.

8.4.2.14   For scientific accuracy, collect and evaluate resources helpful in conducting a scientific investigation.

8.4.3   Using Scientific Instruments and Technology

8.4.3.1   Select and safely use appropriate tools or instruments to complete scientific investigations.

8.4.3.2   Tell how measurements are made using appropriate instruments, including rulers, balances, scales, thermometers, graduated cylinders, and stopwatches.

8.4.3.3   Describe, select, and tell how to use magnifying instruments, including hand lenses, microscopes, and telescopes.

8.4.3.4   Analyze and share data using tools, such as calculators and computers.

8.4.3.5   Tell how technology has led to new careers in science.

8.4.3.6   Tell how inventions, such as the wheel, telephone, and radio, have influenced life and made work easier.

8.4.3.7   Tell how choices regarding the use of technology are influenced by constraints caused by various factors, such as geographic location, limited resources, and social, political, and economic influences.

CHAPTER 5

Information and Activities for Integrating the Faith as Keyed to Grade 8 Standards

The science standards included in this chapter have been compiled from the individual state departments of education and organized, grade by grade, into the following four areas:

1. Physical Sciences

2. Life Sciences

3. Natural Sciences

4. Scientific Processes and Approaches

The standards have been systematized according to the following numerical designations to indicate grade level, area, category, and performance objective as described on the first page of chapter 4.

Performance expectations are numbered sequentially (e.g., the *8* in *2.3.1.8* is found in grade 2, in the natural sciences area, relating to the category of space studies, and is the eighth item in that category.) A complete list of science standards performance expectations for this grade level is provided in chapter 4.

On the pages of chapter 5, which follows, you will find an easy-to-reference two-column format for faith integration with the science standards. The left-hand column under the heading "Information by Topic" provides helpful teaching background information and insights relevant for integrating some aspect of the Christian faith. The number following the topic identifies the performance expectation to which the topic relates (see chap 4). Beside each entry in the right-hand column under the heading "Discussion Points/Activities," you will find helpful ideas for planning and organizing student learning experiences that reinforce and expand upon these faith connections.

Be sure to consult the index at the end of this volume for a complete listing of topics and where they may be found.

PHYSICAL SCIENCES

8.1   Eighth-grade students in Lutheran schools will understand concepts related to the physical sciences.

8.1.1   Composition of Matter

Matter, Classification of

In God's wisdom, He created every kind of matter that living creatures would need, from freshwater rivers and saltwater oceans to soil necessary for many different kinds of plants. Scripture tells us that people were to be good stewards of God's creation (Genesis 1:26). For us to be good stewards of God's creation, we must know about different parts of creation. As you teach lessons on classifying matter, focus on God's wisdom in making different kinds of matter for people to manage and use and the importance of understanding these differences in the world God created. (8.1.1.1)

• Obtain a sample mixture of table salt, sand, and iron filings from the teacher. Observe the mixture in the container, and write down your observations. Next, lay out a sheet of white paper onto the table, and pour the mixture onto the paper. Spread the mixture out evenly. Move a magnet slowly above the mixture. Record the results, and continue separating the mixture until all of the iron filings have been removed from the mixture. Identify the property that allowed the iron filings to be removed from the mixture. Next, pour the remaining mixture into a container of water, and stir for several minutes. Record your results. Then pour the mixture through a coffee filter into another container. Record your results. Describe the properties of sand and salt that allowed the mixture to be separated. Place the salt water container onto the window sill, and let the water evaporate over a period of days. Record your findings. As you work to separate the mixture, consider how God has made every kind of matter unique and how He changed the properties of matter to create the first man and woman (Genesis 2:7, 20–22).

• Using a periodic table of the elements and resource material, compare and contrast properties of the elements by making a taxonomic key of the elements based upon specific properties of matter. List the different categories of elements on your taxonomic key when you are finished, and identify the unique characteristic that sets each category apart. Think about how people are like matter, having similar and distinctly different characteristics. Make a comparison and contrast chart of Cain and Abel (Genesis 4:1–12).

Atoms, Building Blocks of Matter

Scripture tells us that God created all matter. He did so making different compounds from basic particles that we call atoms. Each atom has different chemical properties that make it unique and give it different bonding capabilities. As you teach this lesson on the composition of matter, stress the importance of the atom as the building block in the formation of different substances. Relate this

• The atom is the building block of all substances. Identify the kinds of atoms that make up each of the substances listed, and tell how many of each kind of atom is involved. The substances are sodium hydroxide ($NaOH$), sulphuric acid (H_2SO_4), calcium chloride ($CaCl_2$), table salt ($NaCl$), carbon tetrachloride (CCl_4), oxygen (O_2), carbon dioxide (CO_2), and potassium nitrate (KNO_3). As God is

importance to God's awesome plan and design that separates humans from all other things in His creation (Genesis 1:27–28). (8.1.1.2)

source of all creation, the atom is the source of all substances in creation. Write a paragraph explaining the relationship between the atom and God.

• Using large marshmallows to represent a carbon atom, small marshmallows to represent a hydrogen atom, and toothpicks to represent electron bonds, form the following single-bonded hydrocarbons: C_2H_6, C_3H_8, C_4H_{10}. Record what you notice about the relationships between the carbon atoms and the hydrogen atoms. What is the general formula relating the number of hydrogen atoms to carbon atoms in a single-bonded hydrocarbon? If the pattern holds true, how many hydrogen atoms would be needed to form a single-bonded hydrocarbon with twelve carbon atoms? As you think about atoms as the foundation of substances and the electron bonds that hold them together, reflect on how God is the Creator of all substances, and consider the bond that He has with humanity.

Atoms, Structure of (Protons, Neutrons, Electrons)

Comment that the three subatomic parts of the atom make a great analogy to the Holy Trinity. As God is three persons (John 6:40; 10:38; Matthew 1:18), so also the atom is one entity made up of three distinct subatomic particles: the proton, the neutron, and the electron. (8.1.1.3)

• Draw a diagram showing the location and relationships among protons, neutrons, and electrons for the following elements: lithium, gold, carbon, oxygen, chlorine, and neon. Identify protons with positive charges, neutrons with neutral charges, and electrons with negative charges. After drawing and labeling the diagrams, think about the three persons of God. Draw a diagram showing how God has three distinct persons (Matthew 28:19).

• Draw a Venn diagram showing the three parts of the atom. Label each part of the atom, and tell its charge. Write a paragraph explaining where most of the mass of the atom is located, and explain the relationship between each of the subatomic particles. Next, draw a Venn diagram showing the relationships among the three persons of the Trinity. Inside each part of the Venn diagram, list the Father, Son, and Holy Spirit. Then label the correct person with one of the following characteristics: Redeemer, Sanctifier, or Creator (Galatians 4:5; 2 Thessalonians 2:13; Matthew 19:4).

Elements, Properties and Atomic Structures of

The scriptures show us that God created all of the elements and made creation from substances formed from the elements (Genesis 1:1). Common substances that students use every day are often taken for granted, especially the air that is breathed. But students also take food and drink for granted. God provided all of these things and then allowed the human race to experience His power and wisdom through the complexities of the elements. Stress to students that if one understands the elements, one can then identify a structure upon which new substances may be made from God's creation. (8.1.1.4)

• Research the following elements, and make a list of their properties. Then, organize elements into two different groups based upon the listed properties. The elements are sodium, argon, chlorine, aluminum, carbon, calcium, nitrogen, oxygen, and hydrogen. Write a paragraph explaining what element characteristic was used in separating the elements into the two main groups. Think about how God separated the different parts of creation (Genesis 1).

• Draw an atomic diagram of each of the following elements: sodium, argon, chlorine, aluminum, carbon, calcium, nitrogen, oxygen, and hydrogen. Identify what each of the elements has in common. Then, hypothesize a characteristic of the atomic structure that might be used to organize the given elements. Next, hypothesize how you might create a new element. Design a new element and identify how it differs from the known elements. Tell what you changed and why it makes your element different. Read Genesis 11:3–8, and think about how God changed one characteristic among people and made many different people groups.

Compounds

While Scripture does not speak of compounds by name, a look at the meaning of the word tells us that a compound is a substance united by a firm bond that changes one or more things into something else. God changed many things into new substances throughout Scripture, such as Lot's wife into a pillar of salt (Genesis 19:26), Aaron's staff into a living serpent (Exodus 7:10), and water into wine (John 2: 7–10). Stress that our God is a God of change. Through the Word He changes unbelievers into believers, enemies of God into His children. Nothing is impossible for God. (8.1.1.5)

• Make a list of compounds from labels of products found in the home, such as compounds from medicine bottles, personal items (toothpaste, soap), and cleaning solutions. Then identify the elements in each of the compounds. Use the Internet to go to the Fisher Scientific Web site for help in finding the chemical formula for the substances given. From the list of elements, create as many new compounds (substances) as possible. For instance, if you have an aluminum chlorohydrate compound, which has the elements chlorine, hydrogen, and oxygen, you could construct new compounds of oxygen and water. As you think about constructing new compounds, read about how God makes us all new through Baptism (2 Corinthians 5:17). List the changes that occur when a person is made new in Baptism.

• Compounds are important to life. List the elements bonded together in simple sugars (carbohydrates), proteins, and fats (lipids). Each of these nutrients provides a different benefit to the human body. Research the function of each of these compounds in the human body. Make a list of foods containing these compounds. Think about how God has provided you with all that you need to live and survive. Read Matthew 6:25–34.

Compounds, Properties of

The Lord made His properties known through things He has enabled us to understand. He has shown us His mighty power (Genesis 17:1), His protection (Psalm 33:20), and His care (Psalm 145:8–9). Students know some of the properties of common compounds with which they daily interact, such as soda, water, and bread. Impress on students that each compound has a unique quality as given by God. (8.1.1.6)

• List the properties of a favorite soda, such as taste, color, and so on. From the label of a soda bottle, list the compounds that make soda what it is. Identify each of the elements in the compound, and describe the individual properties of the elements. Then compare how the combined compounds in soda have totally different properties. Read Luke 5:1–11, and hypothesize how fishing for men would take different characteristics and skills than fishing for fish.

• Write the formulas for water, carbon monoxide, carbon dioxide, and table salt. List their common and unique properties and the elements that form the compounds. Then list how each compound is formed. Tell whether the compound is useful or harmful or both. As you think about these common compounds, think about how God controls the properties of water and how He is not bound by them (Matthew 14:22–31).

Molecules

As the atom is the basic unit of matter, the molecule is the basic unit of a compound. Explain that substances consist of numerous molecules of a compound. Scripture tells us that great things begin as small but important units, such as the mustard seed and faith (Matthew 17:20), feeding the five thousand (Matthew 14:16–20), and making the unknown known (Matthew 26:33–34). Comment that God sometimes increases the size of things by increasing the number of basic units. Lead them to understand that they are a unit in God's plan and that their work may also grow to great accomplishments. (8.1.1.7)

• In the list of substances given, identify how many molecules of each substance are present. Then break down the individual molecules into elements and count how many different atoms are present. The substances are $7NaCl$, $5HCl$, and $20Mg(NO_3)_2$. Next, identify which numbers are coefficients and which numbers are subscript numbers. Explain what each number does for the molecule. Read Matthew 14:16–20, and record the basic units of food that were used by the Lord to feed the people. Identify the coefficients for the food, and explain what the coefficients would be increased to feed the people.

• Add different coefficients to the following molecules: H_2O, $MgCl_2$, H_2SO_4, and $Al_2(SO_4)_3$. Next, explain how many molecules are present after adding the coefficients in front of the molecules. Then count the number of atoms of each element, and show how the number of atoms of each element is a factor of the coefficient. Write a paragraph explaining how a molecule of water is the smallest unit of water, and explain how the Earth has oceans that are miles deep. Think about how God exercised His control over both the great and small elements of nature to help the Israelites out of bondage (Exodus 7:14–11:9).

35

Compounds, Properties of

Scripture carefully explains the changes that Jesus' disciples experienced as He took the good qualities in each man and honed those qualities into His plan to spread the Word and its salvation. From fishermen (Luke 5:1–11) to tax collector (Matthew 9:9–13), Jesus chose men who would, with the help of the Holy Spirit, spread the Word through the land. Just as elements give up their individual characteristics as they become compounds, those who follow Jesus give up a sinful nature to walk in God's glory through the sacrifice of Jesus Christ. (8.1.1.8)

• Using the Internet or another resource, identify the characteristics of hydrogen and oxygen. List physical characteristics, such as color, density, and size. Identify the physical characteristics, such as ability to burn. Next, contrast those characteristics with water. Explain how hydrogen and oxygen bond to become the one life-giving substance without which humanity could not survive. Think about how that same water when blessed by God changes us at our Baptism. Read Mark 16:12–18.

• Take a small plastic container, and place a tablespoon of baking soda into it. Record as many observations of the baking soda as you can. Next, observe a container of vinegar. Record as many observations as you can about the vinegar. Next, put a teaspoon of vinegar into the baking soda. Again, record as many observations as possible. Identify whether or not a chemical reaction took place, and support your hypothesis with data from your observations. As you reflect on whether or not a chemical reaction occurred, think about Jesus' disciples and draw an analogy showing how Jesus took quiet, peaceful men and filled them with the Holy Spirit to give them the energy by which He would build His Church. Read Matthew 16:15–20.

Matter, Physical Changes in

Physical changes in a substance alter its appearance without changing any of its chemical properties. Scripture tells us that we are dead to sin but alive to Christ (Romans 6:1–14). In this manner, we are similar to the physical characteristics of matter. When we are baptized, we are dead to sin, but we have not physically changed. We are still the same person. It is only through Jesus Christ's death and resurrection that we will be physically changed at the second coming and have no pain or infirmities. As you teach this lesson, point out that Christians will live a normal life in a normal world, facing all of the challenges that unbelievers face. Remind them that once God (Jesus) took on human form, His physical qualities experienced the same daily living challenges that they face every day. (8.1.1.9)

• Take an ice cube from a cold container and set it in a Petri dish. Using your senses, record as many characteristics as you are able to perceive. Next, put the ice cube in a Pyrex beaker, and place it over a heat source. Observe the changes in its physical appearance. Continue heating the water until it begins to boil. Record your observations as the water boils away. After half of the water has boiled away, remove the beaker from the heat source, and place it into an ice cube tray. Place the tray into a freezer until the next class period. Then take the ice cube tray from the freezer, and record the ice cube. Why is it smaller than before being heated? What happened to the missing matter? As you ponder on where the missing matter has gone, think about what happened after Jesus ascended into heaven. Jesus left us, yet He still remains among us (Matthew 28:20).

• Using a pair of tongs or other tool, take a piece of frozen carbon dioxide (dry ice) and place it in a Petri dish. Observe it for five minutes and record your observations. Next, place the dry ice in a Pyrex beaker of water. Record your observations over the next five minutes. Place the beaker of water containing the dry ice over a heat source. Over the next five minutes, make and record observations. Before placing the dry ice into the water, did it melt? After heating the dry ice, what happened? Do you believe that the dry ice melted as it became smaller? Read Romans 6:1–14, and reflect on how the dry ice departed from the beaker to join the atmosphere where it can be used by green plants. Think about how we are dead to sin but alive to Christ.

Mixtures and Compounds

Jesus tells us that by our own works we cannot achieve the kingdom of heaven (John 14:6). As human beings under the weight of sin (Ecclesiastes 7:20), we are the same as all other human beings around the world. We have the same blood, same organs, and same DNA structures. It is only when we are bonded to Jesus Christ and to others who believe in Him (Ephesians 4:15–16) that we can grow as one body in Christ. As you teach students to analyze the differences between mixtures and compounds, help them to understand the differences between listening to advice from friends and responding. It is different because of the bond God has formed between us and the body of Christ and because the Holy Spirit moves us through Word and Sacrament. (8.1.1.10)

• Observe a container of sand and a container of BBs. Write down your observations. Then, pour thirty BBs into a container of sand. Shake the mixture for three minutes. Devise a mean for separating the BBs from the mixture, using only a piece of paper, a plastic stirrer, and a pair of tweezers. Separate the mixture. Place the ingredients into two different containers after the separation is complete. Read Matthew 25:13–46, and write an analogy comparing the mixture of Christians and nonbelievers to the BBs and sand. Discuss how God will call His own at the time of resurrection.

• Remove five peanut M&Ms from a package. Next, using a scalpel, slice the M&Ms in half. Record your observations. Then, separate the coating and peanut from the chocolate. Hypothesize how you believe the M&M came into being. How was it mixed? Identify the nutrient compounds within the different parts of the mixture. Explain why you cannot physically break down the different nutrients into their component parts. Think about how a baptized Christian is like an M&M, combined spiritually by God so that we may mix (disciple) with one another. Read John 14:15–21.

Chemical Reactions

Scripture tells us that God is capable of making tremendous changes in people as His Holy Spirit work in them through Word and Sacrament. God changed Saul into the apostle Paul on the road to Damascus (Acts 9:1–31). Teach students that chemical reactions cannot be changed back by simple physical means, just as how becoming a Christian changes a person and the person's life and attitude take on different characteristics. (8.1.1.11)

• Using the Internet or another resource, write the chemical structure for the hydrocarbons sucrose, fructose, and maltose. Write the carbon arrangements, and write a paragraph comparing and contrasting the chemical compounds. Read Acts 9:1–31, and think about how God's power works change in a person's life.

• Use the periodic table of elements to find carbon. Make an electron dot diagram, and bond carbon with as many different elements as possible.

List the properties of substances, such as CC_4, CO, and CO_2. Write how these substances are changed by the arrangement of the bonded atoms. Think about how God has changed and continues to change you.

Atoms and the Conservation of Matter

During chemical reactions, one substance is changed into another substance with totally different properties. Before, during, and after the reaction, the number of atoms remains the same, and only their arrangement and bonding are different. Scripture tells us that on the last day we will be changed (1 Corinthians 15:50–54). Point out that believers in Christ are bonded for all eternity and that even death cannot hold us (Romans 8:38–39). (8.1.1.12)

• From a list of balanced chemical equations provided by your teacher, compare the number of atoms of each element on the reactant side with the number of atoms of each element on the product side. Are they the same? What does this tell you about the conservation of matter during a chemical reaction? Think about how God changes us into Christians. After the conversion, are Christians any less? Do they still have two arms, two legs, and one heart? Read Acts 5:12–15, and reflect on the healing powers of God.

• From a list of elements provided by the teacher, make as many different compounds as possible. Count the different elements on each side of the equation. Check with the teacher to determine if your chemical reactions and counts are accurate. Count the number of reactions that contain the same elements. Read Acts 2:14–41, and reflect on how many different combinations of talents were added to the Church by the three thousand converts on Pentecost.

Chemical Reactions, Exothermic and Endothermic

Chemical reactions offer us a medium through which to teach God's omnipotence. Scripture tells us that God is not bound by the physical laws that He created. God controls the flow of energy throughout the world. At various times He caused fire not to burn (Exodus 3:2–3), water to turn to blood (Exodus 7:17), and a storm to become calm (Mark 4:35–41). Impress upon students that we can determine what type of reaction takes place by measuring the energy given off or absorbed, but God can reach far beyond physical laws, and nothing is impossible for Him. (8.1.1.13)

• Take a chemical hand warmer and open the outer package, exposing the warmer to air. For the next fifteen minutes, record the temperature change occurring every three minutes. Look at the package label, and write the active chemical formulas that are causing the temperature change. Identify the type of chemical reaction taking place. Humans have used heat through combustion for many reasons throughout history. Read Exodus 19:18 to learn how God has used combustion (burning) to make His presence known.

• Take a chemical cold pack, read the label, and write the chemical compounds inside. Feel the package, and try to determine which chemical formulas are which. Write a paragraph explaining how you believe the chemical cold pack works. Reflect on how God has given us the knowledge to keep cool during the heat of summer through the use of chemical compounds.

Chemical Reactions, Reactants and Products in

Scripture warns us to be careful regarding our faith and to be wary of false prophets (1 John 4:1; 2 Peter 2:1–4; Mark 13:1–23). Christians need to study Scripture and to be forever diligent as the devil, the world, and our sinful flesh desire to react with us so they may destroy us. Roman 6:23 reminds us that the product of sin is death. Fortunately, the gift of God is eternal life in Christ Jesus, our Lord. (8.1.1.14)

• Take a sheet of paper, and divide it into two columns. From left to right, title the columns "Reactants" and "Products." Then, from a sheet provided by your teacher, divide the chemical reactions by listing the reactants in one column and the products in the other column. Identify each of the substances of the reactant and product on the back of the piece of paper. Think about how important it is to know what the chemical symbols represent and how dangerous it would be to mix the wrong chemicals together. Read Romans 6:23, and write two sets of reactants and products.

• Using the periodic table of elements, construct ten chemical reactions and label the reactants and the products. Identify the type of chemical reactions as being either single replacement reactions, double replacement reactions, synthesis reactions, or decomposition reactions. Think about how important it is to know the different reactions when doing an experiment, and then think about the importance of knowing Jesus Christ as your personal Savior. Read Matthew 16:26.

Solutions, Acidic, Basic, and Neutral

Scripture continually encourages us to resist temptations, and Jesus gave us the perfect example of how to resist Satan (Matthew 4:1–11). For our students to be able to resist Satan, they must receive the power the Holy Spirit offers through Word and Sacrament. As you teach about acids and bases, point out that while solutions can be acidic, basic, or neutral, Christians cannot remain neutral when it comes to sin, because the power of the Holy Spirit works in them through the means of grace. (8.1.1.15)

• Using the Internet or another resource, determine the range of the pH scale. Observe a series of eight containers of common household substances, and hypothesize about which samples are acidic, basic, or neutral. Record your hypotheses in a data table. Test the eight samples of common household substances with litmus paper to determine their pH rating. On the data table, place the substances in the proper category. Read Mark 1:16–17, and reflect on the importance of knowing God and His plan for our lives.

• Research the pH scale, and determine what rating is given to acids and what rating is given to basic or neutral substances. Write a 300–500 word report describing the characteristics of acids, bases, and neutral substances. Hypothesize what would happen if an acid and base of the same strength were placed together. Read 1 Peter 5:8–9, and think about how important it is to know Satan's character and to resist his temptations.

Periodic Table of Elements

Scripture places great importance on characteristics. God gave us the Ten Commandments as a character guide to keep us focused upon what is right (Exodus 20:1–17). Then, He gave us Jesus Christ to fulfill the Law on our behalf (Galatians 4:4–5). Ask students to think about what characteristics separate believers (Christians) from nonbelievers. (8.1.1.16)

• Using the Internet or another resource, research Thompson, Rutherford, Dalton, and Mendeleyev. Write a report on their contributions to the development of the periodic table of elements. On what property is the modern periodic table of elements organized? Read John 10: 25–30, and think about that property on which Christianity is based.
• Using the current periodic table of elements, reconstruct the table according to the atomic mass of each element. Keep the original seven rows and eighteen columns. Then, compare the rearranged elements, and list the elements that are in the wrong columns according to their properties. Think about the properties of the Ten Commandments. Make a chart, and list the characteristics God's Spirit promotes in believers according to each of the commandments.

Metals, Nonmetals, and Noble Gases

Scripture gives us many parables about knowledge and heaven. In the parable of the sower, Jesus talks about spiritual properties conducive to faith development (Matthew 13:1–23). Each part of the parable gives a different set of characteristics and a different set of results. By carefully using things from His disciples' own experience, Jesus helped His disciples grow in their understanding of faith and other spiritual concepts, such as heaven. As you teach about the periodic table of elements, comment to your students about the characteristics that glorify God as they are evidenced among those who are recipients of His saving grace. (8.1.1.17)

• Divide a paper into three columns with the headings "Metals," "Nonmetals," and "Noble Gases." Under each column, write the special characteristics of the elements in each category. Be especially careful to list how each looks, conducts energy, and reacts and its physical strength, and chemical properties. Jesus often used what was known to explain the unknown to His disciples. Read Matthew 13:1–23, and write the characteristics Jesus gave about the people that receive the Gospel. Compare the characteristics of those to the characteristics of the elements on the periodic table of elements. Rewrite the parable using metals, nonmetals, and Noble gases instead of soil.
• Count the number of metals, nonmetals, and Noble gases on the periodic table of elements. Use graph paper to make a coordinate graph for the elements in columns 1–18. Then, make a color-coded key of each element's ability to conduct electricity. Write a paragraph explaining how the graph visually identifies the elements that are able to conduct electricity and their relationship to the periodic table of elements. Then, read about Jesus' disciples, and list their specific characteristics, such as information about their occupations, personalities, and so on. Reflect on how and why Jesus might have picked these men from the many others He might have chosen.

Elements and Isotopes

God knows our hearts. He numbered all our days before even one of them came to be (Psalm 139:16). He calls each one by his or her name (Isaiah 43:1). Even the very hairs on our head are

• Make a poster of one individual element showing its atomic number, common or useful isotopes, and chemical and physical properties. Display posters together with those of your classmates in a promi-

numbered (Matthew 10:30). Just as God knows us completely, what we're made of and what distinguishes us as individuals, so we can understand and identify matter by how it's made. Just as the composition of an atom determines its characteristics and behavior, so we speak (Matthew 12:34) and behave (Matthew 15:18–19) out of the "overflow of our hearts." Our identities can be seen in our speech, behavior, attitude, and witness. (8.1.1.18)

nent location. As you pray together, thank God that He knows us even more thoroughly and individually than we can know each individual element.
• As a class, list properties of an atom and how they relate to that atom's atomic number. Then discuss and list together on the board attitudes and characteristics of the individual person and the behavior by which we can recognize that person.

Atoms, Neutral, Protons and Electrons of

We worship a God of order, and He keeps all things in their proper place and proper balance. Whether we discuss the numbers of petals in monocots and dicots (plants), the repeating valences of elements in the periodic table, or numbers in Scripture, these patterns illustrate the truths God has revealed to us about Himself in His Word. We can learn to recognize these patterns and understand the lessons they hold for us. (8.1.1.19)

• Discuss how patterns appear throughout nature and how we can gain information from them. After investigating patterns in the period table and how Mendeleyev used them to predict undiscovered elements, talk with the class about patterns of numbers in Scripture and their meanings. Choose a number appearing in several Old Testament contexts. Then, based on the use or pattern you find, apply this pattern to one or more New Testament texts. Note what additional understandings of the New Testament text can be gained by understanding number symbolism and patterns in each passage. Common examples include the numbers 7, 10, 12, and 40.
• Suggest examples of balance in nature, beginning with the balance of charged particles in the atom. Other examples might include opposite mathematical functions, Newton's third law, photosynthesis and respiration, bilateral symmetry of many living things, and so on. There is also tension in Scripture. Examples might include saint and sinner, Law and Gospel, and so on. Discuss how the balance or tension between two things is often an essential part of a physical or spiritual truth.

Atom, Mass Number of an

We derive some information from other information. While the number of neutrons in an atom may not be given to us directly, we can find it by working with what we do know, such as the mass number and atomic number, in logical ways like subtraction. Similarly, while Scripture never uses the word *Trinity*, we derive this concept for God by looking at the Scriptures and using the information we are given. (8.1.1.20)

• Find verses identifying each of the persons of the Trinity as God. Review Deuteronomy 6:4, which asserts that there is one God. Write a paragraph explaining the concept of the Trinity, and cite Bible passages that support your statements.
• Examine clear and orthodox statements about the Trinity such as the Athanasian Creed. Discuss how the same sort of inferring we can do to determine the number of neutrons in an atom from the information on the periodic table also underlies the statements in and structure of the Athanasian Creed (e.g., Father is God, Son is God, and Holy Spirit is God, and yet there are not three gods but one God).

Solids, Liquids, and Gases, Differentiation between Atoms or Molecules in

God uses the circumstances of our lives to mold and shape us and to show us His majesty. Whether God is changing us or the world around us, His divine power creates and controls all things so that we might believe in Jesus Christ here on Earth and live with Him eternally. (8.1.1.21)

• We're told in Exodus 14 that a strong wind drove back the waters of the Red Sea so Israel could pass through on dry ground with a wall of water on each side. Point out the astonishing power God displayed in this saving act given the natural properties of liquids and the description given of this event.

• In order to make a bronze statue, the artist must melt the metal into a liquid so he or she can pour it into the mold, so that it will take the shape of its container. In the same way, God softens and melts our hearts so they will take the shape He wants them to have. God wants us to be conformed to His likeness, to the image of His Son (Romans 8:29; 2 Corinthians 3:18; Colossians 3:10). Discuss what it means for a liquid to take the shape of its container and why God must liquefy our hardened hearts in order to transform them.

Molecules

Our heavenly Father is infinitely creative! From a few distinct elements, He makes a near infinite variety of compounds that give our world color, flavor, texture, and substance. God has created a world in which very different things, such as a metal that reacts in water (sodium) and a poisonous gas used to purify water (chlorine), can be chemically combined and create a brand new thing. It is unlike either of the two elements from which it's made and is necessary for our survival; this new thing is salt. As God unites His people in Baptism, in the Lord's Supper, and in faith, He makes them His own and they live for Him, helping, encouraging, and supporting one another in the bond of faith He provides. (8.1.1.22)

• Read Genesis 2:24 and Mark 10:6–9. Just as two atoms combine to become one new substance, we are told that the two people, male and female, become one flesh in marriage. Neither the atoms nor the people lose their individual identities, and yet together they become something more. Discuss ways in which a husband and wife live as one flesh in marriage and how the couple is more than simply two people living together.

• Read about the body of Christ in 1 Corinthians 12:12–31 or Ephesians 5:22–33. Discuss the nature of the Church as the body of Christ—a whole that is "more than the sum of its parts." Discuss how the whole differs from the parts. Compare and contrast that with the joining of atoms to become a molecule. How is the change similar? How is it different?

Protons, Neutrons, and Electrons, Location, Charge, and Mass of

Over the history of chemistry and even particle physics, our understanding of the atom has changed dramatically. Whereas we, like Democritus, once understood it merely to be a single solid object of homogeneous composition, we now know that the three basic particles of protons, neutrons, and electrons are themselves made of other particles. At the other end of the size continuum, we have also come to learn how truly limited our knowledge has been. We've moved from believing the Earth to be the center of the cosmos to realiz-

• Work with your teacher to convert a variety of sizes, such as galaxy and quark, into scientific notation. Construct a room-sized sizeline, as opposed to a timeline, based on the relative sizes of everything from quarks to galaxies. Write them in powers of ten. At appropriate spots on the sizeline, post verses that show God's intimate interaction with His creation at all levels. Examples include Job 9:7–10 and John 2:1–10.

• As you study the model of the atom as it developed over the course of history, reflect on how

ing that the Earth moves around the sun in a solar system, which is part of a galaxy that is itself only part of the larger universe. (8.1.1.23)

scientists' understanding of the atom changed over time, even though the atom itself was the same all along. Connect this to our understanding of creation, pointing out that our limited scientific understanding expands with advancements in science, but creation itself doesn't change. Neither does the Creator! Write a poem to express your gratitude to our unchanging God.

Substances, Classification of

The Bible teaches us about God's absolute command of His creation. This is evidenced, for instance, in Jesus' ability to change even the very substances of which creation is made. Thinking about the stories in Scripture in scientific ways often yields fascinating insights into God's plan of salvation for us and His ability to carry it out. (8.1.1.24)

• Ponder the following questions: How did people know Jesus had changed the water into wine? If Jesus had changed stones into bread, how could someone watching have told the difference? How did people know that the Nile had been turned to blood? The answer to all these questions is by their properties. Explain what a property is and how we use properties to identify and classify substances.

• Working in student lab groups, study pairs of items or pairs of substances mentioned in Scripture. Distinguish between the pairs on the basis of their physical properties. Relevant pairs might include water and wine, bronze and iron, stone and bread, silver and gold, cedar and acacia wood, and so on. For extra credit, find where these substances and their properties are contrasted in Scripture. How were the differences in their properties relevant? (This may be more obvious for some items or substances than for others, so assign accordingly.)

Density

Sometimes understanding Scripture is really a matter of translation. It is not just from one language to another but between cultures, technologies, and mindsets. When we see that we have so much in common with the people of Bible times, it makes it easier to see how the astonishing love of Jesus is every bit as much for us as it was for those people so long ago and so far away. (8.1.1.25)

• Use a table of biblical weights and measures to gain a conceptual understanding of the size of biblical units. Create a chart. In parallel columns, give the metric unit for density (e.g., grams per liter), the English unit for density (e.g., pounds per cubic foot), and a Bible unit for measure (e.g., stones per cubic cubit). In the final column, contrast and compare the three measures.

• Use a table of biblical weights and measures to derive a formula for converting biblical units of density into English or metric units of density. Convert the densities of several common substances from one set of units into the other using the formula you derived.

Density, Calculating

It is a temptation to see the Bible as myth—invented, unrealistic stories—told to explain the unexplainable. However, God's message to us is not a myth. Bibles stories are true and factual! Thinking about the facts of Scripture in practical terms can often help bring home the historical reality of the Word. (8.1.1.26)

• Emphasize the practical reality of Scripture by calculating the density, mass, or volume of various biblical objects. Look up or measure from a sample and calculate the densities of substances such as gold, acacia wood, oil, and so on. Use those densities, along with scriptural descriptions of size, to find the mass of biblical objects.
• Using biblical descriptions of size, show how Scripture's data is realistic. Try calculating things like the estimated mass of Saul's armor (Would it really have been too heavy for David?), the mass of tabernacle furnishings (Could they really have carried them around in the desert for forty years?), and so on.

Buoyant Force

Sometimes it's hard to make familiar stories come alive again, especially for junior high school students. Hands-on construction of replicas engages the students and reinforces the truths of God's saving acts on our behalf. Using the Genesis or Exodus accounts as their guide, have students build models (see column right) in as scripturally accurate a way as possible. Emphasize with them how the Scriptures are trustworthy in all respects. (8.1.1.27)

• Build a model ark, and load it with model animals and people. Weigh your model. Work with your teacher to devise a way to measure the water displaced by their ark. Calculate the weight of the water displaced and compare this to the weight of the model. Build this model with strong materials so you can donate it to younger children for a toy when you are finished with your activity.
• Given biblical data concerning the infant Moses, as a class estimate his weight at the time his mother set him adrift in the basket. Given the density of water, determine approximately how big a basket would have been in order to hold Moses. Individually, in groups, or as a class, find or build a basket large enough to hold such a child. Figure out how to make the basket watertight. Using a doll, weights, and so on, show that each basket would function to hold a baby by trying it out in a lake, river, sink, or tub. Give prizes for the basket with the best stability in the water, the greatest likely historical accuracy, and so on.

Predicting Whether an Object Will Float

Sometimes we hear about miracles in the Bible that go beyond the ordinary expected order of things. Our Lord is sovereign over nature and has demonstrated that lordship over and over in the salvation story, beginning with creation and culminating in the life, death, and resurrection of Jesus Christ. (8.1.1.28)

• Provide dimensions for a typical axe head. Assume this axe head is iron. Calculate its density, and compare it with the density of water. Read the story of Elisha in 2 Kings 6:1–6. Using the relative density of the axe head, explain why Elisha's action is miraculous in scientific terms.
• Read the story of the disciples' miraculous catch of fish in Luke 5:1–11. Build a small boat, and use marbles to represent fish. Using a balance and measurements of volume, have students attempt

to predict how many "fish" it will take to sink the boat. Put the boat into a large container of water, and add marbles one at a time until the boat sinks. Award a prize to the student(s) whose prediction comes closest to the actual demonstration.

Mass and Chemical Reactions

Our God loves each and every one of His children. Not a bird falls to the ground without His knowledge (Matthew 10:29). God truly desires all people to be saved and to come to the knowledge of the truth (1 Timothy 2:4). Even the very hairs on our head are numbered (Matthew 10:30). Every single child of God is known by Him, loved by Him, and preserved by Him. (8.1.1.29)

• In any chemical reaction, however profound the change, not a single atom is lost or destroyed. Similarly, God preserves and protects each of His children, not willing that any should perish. Discuss how God has preserved you through the major changes in your life (John 18:9).
• We have to account for each atom when writing a balanced chemical equation. Talk with your classmates about how God knows us intimately and loves us so much that He will never lose track of us, never forget us, and that Jesus died for each of us individually. Create a poster to underscore this theme.

Motion, Atomic and Molecular, and Temperature

When does God turn up the heat? God turns up the heat on us when He wants movement or change in our lives. As long as we are alive, God's spirit works in us, moving us, prompting us, stirring us to action. When hearts grow cold, they freeze, become rigid, and are hardened. On the other hand, when our hearts are warmed by God, we are moved to action and softened, stirred up, and changed. (8.1.1.30)

• In a class discussion or in writing, share how God has turned up the heat in your life to produce a change in you.
• For classroom devotions, read the story of Moses and Israel's departure from Egypt, and study the person and actions of Pharaoh. Point out that as his heart was hardened, he became more rigid and set in his ways. Read Ezekiel 36:25–26. Lead the class in prayer for yourselves and for others, that God would warm and soften hearts and stir people to greater love and action for each other and for the Lord.

Chemistry and the Functioning of Biological Systems

It is not possible for someone living in the darkness of sin and unbelief to grasp the amazing truths of God's creation. God does that through His divine control over the circumstances of our lives and through the Holy Spirit working through God's Word. Only He can ever break through to bring light to such profound darkness. (8.1.1.31)

• Investigate the notion of intelligent design, highlighting some of the chemical underpinnings of life that are amazingly complex and stunning in their elegance. Praise God for His glory as we see it in even the simplest parts of creation.
• One of the two scientists who received the Nobel Prize for discovering the double helix structure of DNA, Dr. Francis Crick, in his book *Life Itself*, reached the conclusion that such elegant solutions to complex biological problems could not have been achieved through chance over time. However, rather than recognizing the miracles of

creation and concluding that we have an amazing and loving God, Dr. Crick concluded that alien visitors from another planet must have come to Earth and colonized or even designed life as we know it. Pray together that God's Word would break through the darkness for all who are held in unbelief and bring them to faith in Jesus Christ.

Carbon Compounds

As teachers, we know that the most efficient way to reach kids is to adapt to and accommodate their individual strengths and weaknesses, gifts and needs. We don't change the Gospel message or principles of right and wrong, yet we do everything in our power to reach out to and connect with them in the name of Christ. (8.1.1.32)

• Kinesthetically explore the structure of (and possibly reactions of) common organic molecules by having classmates representing atoms link hands or arms to represent bonds between atoms. As you reach out to others to form molecules (or in discussions afterward), note how we as Christians reach out to others with the Gospel. When you are together with your classmates in one particular molecule or set of molecules, pause to pray for those who aren't part of the Church, that someone might reach out to them with the Gospel.

• For devotions, read 1 Corinthians 9:22. Discuss how we can become all things to all people without compromising who we are in Christ. Compare this to the ability of the carbon atom to bond with itself and other elements in so many ways without changing its nature, in other words, while it remains carbon. Point out how as Christians we are called upon to unite both in fellowship with other "Cs" and evangelistic love to other "not Cs."

Organic Compounds

Many of the more complex and useful things in our lives and surroundings are composed of a limited number of components in various combinations. Language is composed of words, which are themselves composed of the letters in the alphabet. Music is composed of various notes with a limited range of pitches and lengths. Paintings are composed of pigments reflecting a very small range of electromagnetic radiation called light. Living organisms are made of a limited set of atoms and primarily of an even more limited set of atoms. Similarly, God has built the unlimited ministry of the Church with a finite set of building blocks. (8.1.1.33)

• Give examples of the huge variety of ways a few elements can combine into the molecules that make up living organisms. Connect this notion with other examples of combinatorial variety in science, language, the arts, and the Church. Examples might include spiritual gifts (Romans 12:3–8), the Scriptures (Ephesians 2:19–22), and so on.

• Read 1 Corinthians 12:1–13 for devotions. Compare the various gifts and types of service to the different atoms in a molecule and the different types of chemical bonds and structures. Talk about the different entities that make up the body of Christ and what it is that binds them to one another to form one whole.

Molecules, Kinds of Organic

Christ's values are not the world's values. Students frequently find themselves caught in the tension between the two. The world would have us believe that people are of little value, especially if there's nothing they have that we want. Paul's message to us in 1 Corinthians 12 stresses the inherent value of every one of us, not only to God but also to one another. Just as a wide variety of molecules are all needed to sustain life, so the enormous diversity of God's people is to be treasured as His gift to the Church. (8.1.1.34)

• Write brief reports on specific molecules or categories of molecules. Reports should include, in addition to other key information, a description of what role the molecule plays in the functioning and well-being of the organism. Also discuss what would happen to living things that contain it if that molecule were suddenly to become no longer available. Read 1 Corinthians 12:14–27, and point out to students that in living things each part, each role, is an essential one. This is true for the individual parts (us) in the living body of Christ, the Church, as well as the separate parts, even the molecules of other living bodies.

• Students often have misguided notions about what makes something important or valuable. For devotions, read 1 Corinthians 12:14–27, and spend a moment considering together what makes a part of the body more or less honorable, more or less presentable, weaker or stronger. As students suggest criteria or biases inconsistent with the truth that every part of the body of Christ is equally important, reason with them using biological comparisons.

8.1.2   Magnetism, Force, and Motion

Gravity

As gravity holds the planets and their satellites in place, Jesus holds sinners close to God through His own righteousness (Matthew 9:12–13). Gravity is a persistent force that never lets up, just as Jesus is always present for us in our time of need (John 12:28; 1 John 1:1–2). As you teach this lesson, show students that gravity is a universal force that is irresistible, and help them to understand that God is master of both gravity and our eternal salvation. (8.1.2.1)

• Gravity is measured by the amount of force it exerts on an amount of mass or weight. The gravity on Earth gives us our weight. As mass decreases so does gravity. Weigh yourself to determine your own weight. Then, figure out what your weight would be if you were standing on the moon. The moon has only one-sixth the gravitational attraction of Earth. Next, figure out what your weight would be on Mars. Mars has 38 percent of the gravitational attraction of Earth. Think about the attraction God has for you. Read 1 Peter 2:4–12.

• Using the Internet or another resource, research the mass and gravitational attraction of the planets and satellites (moons) of our solar system. Using a standard of 100 pounds on Earth, make a data table show how much a 100-pound mass on Earth would weigh on each of the planets and their satellites. Read 2 Peter 3, and reflect on God's great power. Think about what kind of person God desires and equips us to be as He draws us to Himself through the means of grace.

Electromagnets, Role of

In electric motors and generators, electromagnets serve one key function. They convert electrical energy into mechanical energy or mechanical energy into electric energy. How does God's power translate into action in our lives? How do our actions in response to the Gospel encourage others in their life of faith? (8.1.2.2)

• Take a D battery, a length of wire, and a small, handheld magnetic compass. Lay the wire in a straight line directly under the compass and connect it to the battery. Reverse the battery without disturbing the wire and compass, and observe the result. Observe how the flow of electricity produces movement, a reorientation or change of direction of the compass needle. This is much like the Gospel, the power of God for salvation, and how it produces movement or change in us and reorients our will to bring it into alignment with God's will. Discuss how this is a simple example of an electromagnet converting electrical energy to mechanical energy.

• Bring in a flashlight you shake or hand crank to provide power rather than replacing batteries. Make sure you have mostly or completely drained it so the light is dim or off. For devotions, ask what it means for us to let our light shine (Matthew 5:16). Discuss how God is telling us that our actions in faith become a light others can see. Turn on the flashlight (previously drained), and explain that our actions are like shaking (or cranking) the flashlight—the electromagnet inside transforms that mechanical energy into electrical energy. When we do things that please God and serve others, we shine and bring glory to our heavenly Father. Pray that God would empower each of you to let the light of God's glory shine brightly into the dark world around you.

8.1.3   Energy

Motion and Distance

Scripture tells us that God sees time differently from people (2 Peter 3:8). God is the Creator of the vast distances of the universe (Genesis 1:1). The definition for movement is a change in position over a measurable period of time. In order to complete His plan for the salvation of humanity, God breached the distance between sin and redemption (the fall and resurrection) over a long period of time in human history, but this time period was according to His plan. Stress that God has moved us past sin and closed the distance between fallen humanity and salvation. (8.1.3.1)

• Using a scaled road map or other resource, determine how long it would take to drive from New York to Los Angeles if a team of drivers could do so at 60 miles per hour without refueling or stopping. Then refigure the time it would take if you increased your speed by 10 percent, 12 percent, and 15 percent. Reflect on the circumstances in life that sometimes bring us closer to God and those that distance us from Him. What conclusions can you make looking at the lists?

• On your trip to school, calculate the time and distance you traveled to school. Also keep track of the directions that you were traveling in relationship to the cardinal directions of north, south, east, and west. Write a paragraph explaining whether or not you would reach school sooner if you could drive in a straight line. Be sure to support your opinion with facts. Read James 1:1–15, and reflect upon the importance of position in our relationship with God. What suggestions does James provide for those concerned about the trials and temptations that distance believers from God?

Motion, Accelerated and Constant

Scripture tells us that the Israelites often had little patience while waiting for the completion of God's plan for redemption. They didn't open their hearts and minds to the Holy Spirit and often turned away from God. Even the disciples had trouble understanding the speed of God's plan (Acts 1:1–8). As you teach about acceleration, comment on God's timing and the appropriateness of the speed at which He accomplishes His will. (8.1.3.2)

• The definition for acceleration tells us that both speed and direction are involved. Because speed is figured by the relationship between time and distance, constant acceleration requires either the speed or direction to be continually changing at equal intervals. On the back of ten large index cards, write up five mathematical problems that demonstrate constant motions and five mathematical problems that demonstrate accelerated motion. After completing the problems, exchange them with another student, and work through the answers. Check for accuracy. As you think about accelerated motion, consider the growth of Christianity. What is the driving force behind that growth? Read Matthew 28:16–20.
• Collect a long balloon, a soda straw, a 15-foot length of string, and some tape. Cut the soda straw in half, and tape it to the balloon. Blow up the balloon and hold the nozzle tight to prevent air from escaping. Next, put the string through the soda straw. Have a partner hold one end while you hold the other and the balloon. Have a third person with a stopwatch observe the balloon as you release the nozzle. Record the time and distance on a data sheet. Repeat the process several times, putting different amounts of air in the balloon each time. Determine the speed of each run. Was there a constant motion or acceleration taking place? Think about the Israelites as God brought them out of Egypt. Was their journey at a constant pace, or were there times of acceleration? Read Exodus 14. Think about your relationship with your heavenly Father. Is your faith life moving along at a constant speed at this time, or is it accelerating? Why?

Acceleration, Speed and Time

While the unfolding of God's plan for salvation began immediately after Adam and Eve ate the forbidden fruit (Genesis 3), it accelerated rapidly after Jesus' birth. It moved slowly from Adam to Noah, from Noah to Moses, from Moses to King

• Take a marble and a wooden ruler with a trough in it (or other object with similar capabilities), and place the ruler at a shallow angle. Put the marble on the ruler, and using a stopwatch, allow the marble to roll down the ruler. Measure the time it

INFORMATION BY TOPIC

DISCUSSION POINTS/ACTIVITIES

David, from King David to John the Baptist, and from John the Baptist to Jesus but clearly began to gain speed toward the end. As you teach this lesson, explain that speed is directly related to time. Remind students that time can be judged from many perspectives. A second can be a long time if you are touching something hot, while a holiday break may seem to go by very quickly. (8.1.3.3)

takes. Calculate the acceleration of the object. Repeat the process three times. Increase the angle of the ruler by ten degrees, and repeat the entire process. What relationship is there between the amount of incline and the rate of acceleration? Reflect on how God has created Earth (Genesis 1) in such a manner that it revolves around the sun at a certain speed and rotates on its own axis at a certain speed. Write a hypothesis of what might happen if Earth stopped rotating on its axis.

• Take a small wheeled metal toy car and a flat wooden board (or other object with similar capabilities), and place the board at a shallow angle. Put the car on the board, and using a stopwatch, allow the car to roll down the board and measure the time it takes. Calculate the acceleration of the object. Repeat the process three times. Increase the angle of the board by ten degrees, and repeat the entire process. What relationship is there between the amount of incline and the rate of acceleration? Read Mark 16:15–20, and then calculate the possible acceleration of Christianity if two people become Christians one day and then each converts another person the next day. The four Christians each convert another person the next day. Calculate the rate of acceleration and determine how many new Christians would be added to the Kingdom by the end of a thirty-day month.

Reference Point and an Object's Change of Position

Scripture continually reminds us that position is important to the Christian. As God's Spirit moves us from our own desires to follow the plan that God has devised for us, our perspective and being are continually changing and evolving (1 Corinthians 6:11). Growing in Christ often makes us leave our comfortable lives behind to do His bidding (Matthew 9:9). As you teach this lesson, stress that we may enter the kingdom of God as a small child (Matthew 18:2), but as God's Spirit nurtures us through Word and Sacrament, we are enabled to grow in our faith and understanding (1 Peter 2:2–3). (8.1.3.4)

• Pair up with a partner, and sit at a table or desk facing each other. Place on the table three objects of different sizes. Place the objects in a row. Then, tell your partner to move the object on the right forward. If your partner asks for clarification, simply repeat the instruction without telling your partner whether or not you mean your right or your partner's right. Write down your partner's choice. Get another partner, and repeat the process. What have you learned about motion? Did all of your partners make the same decision? Read Matthew 14:22–33, and explore Peter's perspective of Jesus as he steps from the boat. Notice how Peter reacts as his focus changes from Jesus to the waves.

• Take a piece of clear, hard plastic or unbreakable glass, and place a quarter on it. Then, working with a partner, lift the coin to eye level. Have your partner observer the coin from beneath while you observe the coin from above. Record as many observations as possible. Discuss the similarities and differences. Write a paragraph on how your perspective was different from your partner's. Write a paragraph about how your life's perspective would be different if you were on the moon. Read Matthew 16:21–23, and reflect on how Jesus' death can be looked at as both horrible and wonderful at the same time, because it allowed the fulfillment of Scripture, Jesus' resurrection, and our salvation.

Motion

While humanity has been constantly headed in the direction of its own destruction from the time of the fall, God put into effect a plan to change that direction (1 Peter 1:3–12). Without God intervening and setting us off into the right direction, we would be hopelessly lost to follow Satan's path (John 14:6). Stress that motion is a change in direction and that the correct direction for the Christian is the one in which God's Spirit propels us as He changes and empowers us through Word and Sacrament. (8.1.3.5)

• Working in teams of two, one person with a watch or stopwatch, take a tour around the playground and school hallways. Count off the steps, and time your walk in each direction. Mark the time and distance of each leg of the trip. Then, back in the classroom, calculate the speed of each leg of the journey. What was the longest leg? What was the fastest leg? Was the fastest leg also the shortest leg? What was the average speed overall? Time is an essential part of determining the rate of change in position. Read Ecclesiastes 3:1–8, and reflect on how God has a time for everything and that time changes our position. Read Psalm 31:15a. Comment on these words and what they mean to you.

• Using a map of the area in which you live, plot out the direction from your house to the grocery store, to the nearest movie theatre, to the doctor's office, to the post office, and to the nearest department store. Then, calculate the time it would take you to reach each of those locations. Identify the cardinal direction you would use to begin the journey. Read Psalm 107:3. From which direction will God gather those He has redeemed? How far and in which direction has God removed our sins (Psalm 103:12)?

Unbalanced Force, Actions of an, and Changes in an Object's Direction

Scripture tells us to lead a balanced life, being sure to plan time to worship the Lord (Exodus 20:8–11). When we fail to keep God in our lives, we become unbalanced and stumble. Newton points out in his laws of motion that when unbalanced forces oppose each other, movement will be in the direction of the greater force. Emphasize that we are unbalanced when we keep our faith hidden. Help students understand the strength God promises to impart to His people through the means of grace. See John 15:5. (8.1.3.6)

• Partner with another student approximately your own size. Stand with your partner. Move to a distance where both of you can easily put the palms of your hands together. On a count of three, both of you push against each other at the same time. What happened? Did you move farther backwards than your partner? If not, why? If so, why? Repeat the process with someone much larger and someone much smaller. Record the results. Then, read Matthew 17:20, and reflect on the power God promises to those who have faith.

• Take a piece of paper, and fold it into a paper airplane. Find a place where you can fly the airplane. Measure how far it flies. Repeat the process by changing the size of the wings. Did the airplane fly farther or not? What are the opposing forces of flight? By changing the wings, what set of forces did you change? Read John 19:28–37, and reflect on the death and resurrection of Jesus Christ. What force did Jesus oppose? What was the outcome of these unbalanced forces?

Waves and Energy

Scripture warns us of Satan's power (Acts 26:15–18). Satan never runs out of energy, and he uses his power to turn us from God. As waves transfer energy (sound waves, ocean waves, Earth waves, and radiation), Satan transfers his energy through our own selfish desires. Warn students not to take Satan lightly. Just because we cannot see Satan doesn't mean that he isn't actively trying to keep us from God. (8.1.3.7)

• Design a model of a sound wave or an ocean wave, and label the parts of the wave. What characteristic of a wave tells how powerful the wave is? What characteristic of a wave tells the frequency of the wave? Read Acts 26:15–18, and compare Satan to a wave. How does Satan use his energy? What is Satan's purpose?
• Compare a sound wave to an ocean wave. How are they similar? How are they different? Which wave has more power? Why? A sound wave cannot be seen, but an ocean wave can be seen. Do they both transfer energy in the same manner? Read Acts 26:15–18 and John 3:16, and compare the energy Satan transfers to humankind to the transfer of energy God gives to humankind. Create a poster illustrating the transfer of God's redeeming grace as described in Psalm 51:10–13.

Vibrations and Waves

Scripture tells us that God has used earthquake waves to demonstrate His power (Matthew 27:51). God also sends out His power in other ways. Like pebbles dropping in a pond, God spreads His Holy Spirit among us, building up our energy and zeal to do His will (Romans 8:9). As you teach about vibrations and energy disbursement, focus on how God's Word spreads out in all directions and adds Christians to His kingdom (1 Timothy 2:4). (8.1.3.8)

• Pour water into a deep plastic washbasin. Take a small marble and drop it into the water. Record the wave and how it spreads out. Next, drop a medium-sized marble into the water. Record data for that wave. On the third attempt, drop a large marble into the basin. Again, record the results. Which wave had the greatest energy? Which wave had the least energy? What is the physical relationship between the energy of the waves and the marbles that were dropped? Read Matthew 28:19, and reflect on the pebbles that God drops among us with His Holy Spirit. How do those waves spread Christianity?
• Pour water into a deep plastic washbasin. Drop one marble into the water, and record the wave disbursement. Drop two marbles of the same size into the water at one-second intervals. Record the wave disbursement. Repeat the process with three, four, and five marbles. How does the energy from multi-

ple marbles being dropped into the basin compare with the single drop? Read Matthew 4:18–22, and reflect on how God built His Early Church by sending out the disciples. Compare that process with the energy spread out by multiple marbles being dropped and reflect on how God's Word is spread each time we use it to further His plan.

Molecular Motion, Conduction and Convection Based on

Scripture tells us that the apostles were personally called by Jesus (John 1:35–42; Acts 9:1–19). These apostles spread the Word and made many disciples, which in turn have been making disciples for Christ for generations. As you teach about conduction and convection, compare the terms to sharing of the Gospel by the apostles and disciples of Jesus. While conduction means direct encounter, convection currents spread out over a great distance to give energy to objects not in direct contact with the original source. (8.1.3.9)

• On a piece of poster board, draw a model of energy conduction and energy spread through convection currents. Be sure to label each part of the models, and show how energy is transferred with each model. Read John 1:35–42 and Acts 9:1–19, and reflect on the power that direct contact with Jesus Christ had on His apostles. Think about how God has contacted and empowered you.

• Using the Earth as a model, show how the sun's energy is absorbed by the Earth and then conducts heat (daytime heating) into the air long after the sun sets. Next, show how the Earth's atmosphere warms from contact with the Earth's surface and then spreads energy through convection currents to other areas. Read Acts 6:1–7, and reflect on how God's Word works like a convection current, spreading Christianity throughout humankind. Review the concept of apostolic succession. Which is most like apostolic succession: conduction, convection, or both?

Radiation

Make a connection with the means by which God's Word, His messages of Law and Gospel, come to us. In convection, currents of air or other fluids pick up heat from a source and carry it to places with less heat. In the same, we take God's Word from an environment that is rich with it and bring it to those who need to hear it. How often do you share the Gospel with those around you? (8.1.3.10)

• Make an analogy between conduction, convection, and radiation and the ways in which God's Word reaches us. Radiation might be compared to God speaking directly to us through the Scriptures. In this way we take in God's messages of Law and Gospel directly. Conduction might be compared to the Sacraments, where God uses physical elements as means of grace to convey His saving Word to us. How might God's people, actively sharing the Gospel, be compared to convection?

• Consider the words *means*, as in means of grace, and *medium*, as in matter through which or by means of which something is transmitted. Discuss various contexts in which we would call something a means or a medium. Distinguish between the two. With the class, develop a table that outlines the transmission process. Include four columns entitled "Source," "Transmission," "Means or Medium," and "Receiver." Share with examples from what you and your classmates have studied this year. Examples might include sound; light; heat (all three methods); God's Word; information transfer in art, music, or history; the transfer of money in an economy, and so on. When there is no means or medium, write "none." Tell whether each involves a means, a medium, both, or neither.

Conduction, Convection, and Radiation, Ways to Reduce

Science almost inevitably leads to its application: engineering. Students will better understand science when they must apply it, and they will better understand the Scriptures when they apply God's Word in the life they live for Him. (8.1.3.11)

• Shadrach, Meshach, and Abednego were thrown into a blazing furnace but were miraculously saved by God. Since we don't have the ability to direct God's power over all aspects of creation, how might we go about protecting something from intense heat? Work in teams to assume the following challenge: Devise a way for an egg to survive in a hot oven for a specified length of time without cooking. At the end of the specified trial period, remove each egg from the oven, and crack it onto a room temperature plate to compare how much each egg has cooked. Award a prize to the team with the least-cooked or coolest egg.
• The soldiers who threw Shadrach, Meshach, and Abednego into the furnace died from the heat. How do you think the hot furnace killed them? How might someone working around an extremely hot furnace today protect himself? If possible, interview people whose jobs require them to work in very hot environments to find out how they stay safe.

Energy, Forms of

Holy Scriptures contain a wealth of examples we can draw from in teaching students about the natural world. God not only created the tangible, scientific world we live in, but He also came to be in that world in the flesh—God with us (Isaiah 7:14). Studying the Scriptures in all their down-to-Earth reality can help bring home the profound mystery and yet absolute reality of the incarnation. (8.1.3.12)

• Identify the type of energy indicated in each of the following Bible verses: Matthew 2:10 (light or radiance); John 2:1–11 (chemical); Matthew 24:27 (electric); Acts 2:2 (acoustic); Acts 16:26 (mechanical); Mark 14:67 (thermal).
• Visit a church sanctuary to identify various forms of energy that can be found there. Examples include chemical energy in the elements of Communion and in fuels such as wax or oil; light from the sun, fixtures, or candles; sound from the organ, piano, or other instruments; electricity for lights; heaters; a screen that moves up or down; or the action inside a piano as someone plays.

Heating and Cooling

What is hell? One definition explains hell as separation from God. Just as dark is the absence of light and cold is the absence of heat, so the worst possible punishment is the absence of God. (8.1.3.13)

• Take on the challenge of creating darkness in your well-lit classroom. As you work, reflect on how darkness is nothing more than the absence of light. Nothing emits darkness. Extend this idea of defining one thing as the absence or lack of something else to heat and cold and to heaven and hell.

• Why do you wear a coat outside in the winter? (To keep the heat in.) Why do you often get soft drinks in insulated cups? (To keep the heat out.) Discuss how warmer things share their heat energy with cooler things. Discuss how we are sometimes like a thermos, creating hell (or separation from God) for ourselves or others by not allowing the heat of His Word to penetrate and bring its energy into our lives. What things insulate us from God's grace in our lives? As a class, pray that God would make each one a conductor of God's grace, not an insulator.

Energy Derived from Renewable Resources

One way we honor God is by treating the world He has made—His creation—with respect, protecting it, nurturing it, and living in it responsibly. When we consume our earthly resources faster than they can be renewed, we are exploiting that creation rather than respecting it. On the other hand, it is always our Creator God who renews our faith and strength. (8.1.3.14)

• As a class or in teams, design and build a useful device that runs on a renewable power source such as the force of moving water, wind, solar radiation, or the activity of people. Operate the device at least once. Discuss how with more technological resources such a device might be made more efficient. Discuss how this device honors God by assisting in the preservation of the resources in God's creation.

• For classroom devotions, lead the class in a Bible study about how God provides all we need and renews us. You might read and discuss such passages as Psalm 103:5; 2 Corinthians 4:16; Psalm 51:10–12; and Isaiah 40:28–31. Note how He has provided the wind and the sun for our physical needs, God also renews our spirits using a source of power we can never exhaust—the means of grace!

Circuits, Simple and Parallel

God gives us gifts and resources, such as our minds, our time, technology, and so on, so we can use them to bring Him glory and share the Gospel with others. A study of science applied in engineering and technology provides a perfect opportunity to exercise stewardship of our intellectual and technological gifts with our students and parents. (8.1.3.15)

• Design and build a simple game show set to be used for a school or church festival, a local carnival, an open house, a chapel skit, a talent show, and so on. Include a switch and a light, buzzer, or other signaling device for each player. Also include decorative lighting, sounds, and the like, to add interest to the presentation. Develop a game that makes a point in a chapel skit, serves as a vehicle for sharing the Gospel, or encourages study of the Scriptures by rewarding knowledge of the Bible.

• Design and build a puppet theater complete with lighting and other theatrical helps such as motorized curtain draws or sound effects. Use it to share Bible stories with younger children in classrooms, chapel worship, or other settings. At the end of the year, donate it to your (or another) congregation or ministry group, along with handmade puppets, student-written scripts, and so on, to help them establish a puppet ministry.

Energy, Change and Constancy of

We worship an unchanging God. Throughout all the ages of history and all the ages of our lives, our God loves and sustains us. No matter what else happens in our lives—heaven and Earth themselves could pass away—and yet God's Word will never pass away (Matthew 24:35). Throughout our life and to its end, God will sustain and save us. His Word, His love, and His unchanging nature have been from before time was created and will endure until time itself passes away. (8.1.3.16)

• Consider the series of energy transformations (e.g., burning a log, snapping a rubber band, driving a car) your teacher will present to you, beginning with very simple ones found in closed systems and stepping up to more complex, open systems. Follow the transfer of energy, showing how through every change the energy remains constant. God is like that. In every change, He will remain faithful. Reflect on God's constant love for you as you read portions of Psalm 136 and sing the beloved hymn "Be Still My Soul."

Energy Transformation in a Simple Closed System

Our God changes things and changes people. Throughout history and throughout Scripture, we see the Lord changing the natural world, human history, and hearts, minds, bodies, and spirits. On the Last Day, we and all believers will be transformed. "He who was seated on the throne said, 'I am making everything new'" (Revelation 21:5). (8.1.3.17)

• Use scientific ideas and terms to describe events recorded in the Scriptures. Create a game, worksheet, or other activity for students where through matching, short answer, or a brief response, they can identify events in the Bible according to the energy transformations to which they most closely relate. Sample passages might include Luke 3:9 (chemical to radiant light); Revelation 3:20 (mechanical to acoustic); Psalm 77:18 (electrical to radiant); John 3:8 (mechanical to acoustic); Psalm 29:7–9 (acoustic to mechanical).
• In classroom devotions, study Romans 12:2; 2 Corinthians 3:18; and Philippians 3:20–21. What does it mean to be transformed? Begin with the root words *trans* and *form*. Connect this to energy and other transformations. How are we being transformed right now? What evidence can we find to show that this transformation is taking place? What is "His likeness" into which we are being transformed? Who is doing the transforming? How is being transformed different from merely conforming?

8.1.4 Simple Machines

Simple Machine Compared with Joints of Human Body

In order to make work easier, God provided humans with the wisdom to make tools (Genesis 4:20–22). He also placed us in charge of His creation (Genesis 2:15). Remind students that God has given us the knowledge to make tools so that we can use them to do the work He would have us do. Comment that God created the concept of simple machines and incorporated them into His design of the human body. (8.1.4.1)

• Study a chart showing the joints of the human body. List each joint separately. Compare each joint with one or more simple machines. Write a paragraph on each comparison, and explain the similarities. Then, write a paragraph about the importance of the machines in our daily lives. Reflect on how God has given us the ability to use machines to make work easier. Think about the responsibility that God has entrusted to us. Read Genesis 2:15.
• Compare a lever to a hinge joint. Identify where the effort force is when using a lever and where it is in relationship to the human elbow. Then, repeat the process with the neck joint, and compare it to a screw. Make a list of simple tools that you have used in the past few weeks, and write two or three paragraphs explaining how God has made your life easier by designing His creation to include these simple machines.

Simple Machines, Functioning of

Consider the fact that God could do anything and everything more efficiently alone! So why doesn't He? Why did Jesus make the people He calls "Church" His body in the world? Why not do it all Himself? Think about how you're teaching your students who take longer and are slower than you are. Why do you bother? Isn't it because you love them and want them to mature? Make the analogy that the Church is like a complex machine, which is a combination of many simple machines (people) with each doing a particular needed task that makes the whole (Church) function. (8.1.4.2)

• Work equals force times distance. Most simple machines increase the distance so you can decrease the force. Consider that distance equals the days of your life. Work equals the task God preordained for you to do. Force equals the strenuous effort factor. When God grants a person a specific number of days of life and that person puts in strenuous effort, then a great deal of valuable work is done in the Kingdom. Examine your own life in terms of work.
• Machines make work easier either by multiplying force, multiplying distance, or changing direction. We aren't machines, but we can accomplish what a machine does because our bodies are set up with levers in the arms, wedges in the teeth, wheel and axles at the hips, and so on. In groups, trace someone's outline on large paper. Now draw in various bones, tendons, muscles, teeth, inner-ear parts, and other things that use simple-machine principles. Label each by writing down which of the three ways it makes work easier. Who invented "machines" first?

8.1.5   Sound

Sound, Travel of

The Scriptures give many examples of the importance of sound. Sound announced God's presence to Adam and Eve in the garden of Eden (Genesis 3:8) and to Moses and the Israelites at the foot of Mt. Sinai (Exodus 19:16). God used sound to demonstrate His mighty power at the wall of Jericho (Joshua 6:20). Jesus uses the characteristics of sound to describe the Holy Spirit to Nicodemus (John 3:8). A mighty wind was heard at Pentecost (Acts 2:2). Guide students to understand that God uses the known to explain the unknown and that God is often like sound, impossible to see but always felt or realized. (8.1.5.1)

• Sound travels by vibrations that cause energy to be transmitted through some medium in the form of waves. Fill several containers with water. Then, strike different size tuning forks or other pieces of material that vibrate at different frequencies against the table-top and place them into the water. Write down the results. Pay special attention to how invisible sound waves are transferred into visible waves in the water. God tells us in His Word that the resurrection of the body will be accompanied by the sound of the trumpet (1 Corinthians 15:52). What change will take place at this time?

• Cut a hole in the bottom of two small plastic cups. Attach two paper clips to each end of a 10-foot piece of twine. Insert the paper clips into the holes in the cups, and turn them sideways. Stretch the lines tight. Have one person talk into one cup while another person listens through the cup at the other end. Using the wave model, record your explanation of the ability to hear sound at the other end. Reflect on how God uses various aspects of the nature of sound as a metaphor for the ways He speaks to us (Job 26:14). Many times God used the sound of the trumpet in Scripture to announce His coming (Exodus 19:19). Identify how sound waves are produced by musical instruments, and explain how the instruments change the frequencies of sound waves to make different tones. Why are trumpets often played at Easter Sunday worship services? See also 1 Corinthians 15:52.

Sound, Characteristics of

Compare the speed of light in air, which is 186,000 miles per second, and of sound in air 346 miles per second, to the speed of light in water, 140,000 miles per second, and of sound in water 1,531 miles per second. How do these differences affect the animals in the food chain above and below the waterline? For example, how many hertz does an elephant hear (3) compared to a dolphin (50)? Sometimes we take the difference between sight and sound for granted, but pause and wonder how different it would have been if God reversed those speeds. (8.1.5.2)

• Cut off both ends of a small juice can. Cut open a balloon, and stretch it over one end. Secure with a rubber band. Glue a 1/2-inch square fragment of a mirror slightly off center. Darken the room. Place the can near a dark wall. Shine the beam of a flashlight so it bounces off the mirror and reflects onto the wall. Have someone speak softly into the open end of the can. Try shouting, whistling, and singing. Observe the length of the bouncing light's reflection. What effect does pitch make? What effect does volume make? From this observation, take a guess at how the eardrum works as it connects to neurons. Marvel that we are wonderfully made as Psalm 139 says. Also consider being good stewards of your ears.

• Research the following strange facts about sound waves: (1) the uses we're making of sound right now, such as to create sound pictures or sonograms, to quicken chemical reactions in the manufacture of drugs and plastics, to create bubbles in cleaning solutions that eventually cause shock waves to vibrate dirt off delicate lab instruments; (2) how temperature affects the ability to hear, just like cool night air makes sound more audible to the human ear; (3) how we detect sound in outer space, such as the fact that sound can't travel through empty space; (4) surprising tidbits, such as pigeons can distinguish the difference between composers. Let students put their findings on a monthly bulletin board titled "Complex Creations" with the feature this month as "Sound."

• Sound needs a medium to travel through to connect the source to the receiver. Jesus is the medium connecting us to God and vice versa. He set up the system and keeps it operating by using prayer as the vibrations. In your list of powerful invisible things like love, sound, and angels, include prayer.

8.1.6 Light

Light, Reflection, Absorption, and Refraction of, and Shadows

Scripture gives us direct evidence of God's power as He provided the world with light. God tells us that light is good (Genesis 1:3). He also indicates that shadows or darkness are the opposite of light (John 3:19–21) and that we should be careful to always walk in the light (1 John 1:7). The reflection of light gives us an ability to see ourselves in a mirror, and the refraction of light allows us to see things that we cannot see with the naked eye. Point out the importance of growing in knowledge and that as God allows us to advance in skills, He also reveals more of His power and majesty to us. (8.1.6.1)

• God gave us light in the universe and separated Earth's darkness by giving us daylight and moonlight (Genesis 1:14–16). Cover two different size balls with aluminum foil. Place the balls close to each other. Then in a darkened room, shine a flashlight at the smaller object. Write what you notice about light. Did the light striking the larger object reflect to the smaller object? Write a paragraph explaining how the flashlight acted like the sun and provided light, while the smaller object acted like the moon and did not produce light but simply reflected the light.

• Using the objects from the first activity, place the smaller ball directly in front of the larger ball, and shine the light straight at the smaller ball. Write what you see, especially how certain parts of the larger ball are cast in shadows. Using this concept, explain how you cast different shadows at different times of the day when you are out in the sunlight. Explain how God is different from the shifting shadows (James 1:16–17).

• Bring in several small pictures of animals. Use concave and convex lenses to observe the animals. How did the animal change with the concave lenses? Feel the shape of the concave lenses, and write an explanation of how the shape of the lenses changed the direction of the light rays. Next, do the same thing with the convex lenses. Using this information, explain how a telescope is used to see things far away. Explain how much of what we see about God is a reflection and that when we see God face-to-face our eyes will be opened (1 Corinthians 13:12).

Colors in the Spectrum

By way of a rainbow, God used color to give us a permanent visual reminder of His covenant to us (Genesis 9:13). Throughout Scripture, colors are used to signify beauty. King David's gifts for building the temple were colorful stones (1 Chronicles 29:2). Colors have also been used to show affection, such as Israel's gift to Joseph that eventually contributed to Joseph's being sold into slavery (Genesis 37:3). As you teach this lesson, stress how God let light be affected by the different gases on Earth and throughout the universe. He also let light become a tool for opening our eyes to knowledge, such as being able to determine the atmospheres of the other planets in our solar system by reading the light spectrum of those planets. (8.1.6.2)

• God placed a rainbow in the sky as a sign of His covenant between Himself and humanity. Research reference materials and draw a picture demonstrating this covenant. Use all of the colors of the spectrum. Write an explanation about the wavelength for each color. Reflect on God's covenant with humanity (Genesis 9:13).
• Using reference materials to help determine the wavelengths of different colors, make a rainbow as it would appear on either Venus or Mars. Write a paragraph explaining why a rainbow on Venus or Mars would look different from one on Earth. Explain what God has given Earth that makes a rainbow such an important covenant (Genesis 1:7).

Color, Differences in

Many animals see only in black and white even though the world exists in color. Many people see life in black and white too. Everything is either right or wrong, and rules must be upheld and even more written up to be sure the first ones aren't broken. By the time of Jesus, the teachers of the law and Pharisees had 613 rules developed from the initial ones. When Jesus healed on the Sabbath, they accused Him of working, one of those many prohibitions. Jesus rebuked these people. A law focus generally leads to either awareness of sinfulness with repentance or self-sufficient righteousness with blindness to sinfulness. Jesus saw in color and still does. Race, economic condition, gender, and age do not matter. Jesus offers His love and mercy to all. He is not a black-and-white Savior. That's good news particularly for Gentiles like most of us. (8.1.6.3)

• Introduce this concept by mixing the primary paint colors to get a muddy gray. Mix the primary colors of light using transparent colored cellophane over flashlights to get white. Explain what happened. (Every light wave is absorbed by the paint and none are reflected back so you get black. When all the colors are blended, you get what the prism has before the waves are refracted.) Some people think good and evil are balanced forces. They think God created evil, because otherwise how could evil exist since God created everything? Thus God is really to blame for evil. The demonstration shows a different way to look at things. Darkness is what happens in the absence of light. Evil is not created; it happens when pure light isn't reflected.
• Pass out pairs of flashlights covered with colored cellophane. What do you expect to happen when you combine the two? For example, green and red light combine to make yellow. Hypothesize why God made leaves green (chlorophyll absorbs yellow and red, reflecting back green). What colors are most abundantly produced by our sun (yellow and red)? Is this coincidence or design?

LIFE SCIENCES

8.2   Eighth-grade students in Lutheran schools will understand concepts related to the life sciences.

8.2.1   Plants and Animals

Organisms, Classification of

Living organisms can be classified many different ways. The modern classification system has five kingdoms: Monera, Protista, Fungi, Plantae, and Animalia. These kingdoms separate organisms based upon distinct differences. Scripture separates the Christian from the non-Christian by one important characteristic: salvation through Jesus Christ (Mark 16:16; Romans 8:1–11). As you teach about classifying living things, remind students that Christians delight in sharing the same characteristic that grants them eternal life (John 5:24–27). (8.2.1.1)

• Make a list of ten different organisms. List the characteristics that the organisms have in common. Next, place organisms with similar characteristics together. Identify to which kingdom the organisms would belong. Continue classifying the organisms down through the system until all of the organisms are separated. What did you learn about the classification system as you moved farther away from the kingdom level? Read 1 Corinthians 12:3–5, and think about the things that unite and divide the followers of Christ.
• Moving down the classification system from kingdom to species, write two or three sentences to explain the identifying characteristic shared by organisms at each level. At the lowest level (species), how many different types of organisms share the same level? Read Mark 16:16 and Romans 8:1–11, and identify what distinguishing characteristic is shared by all Christians.

Plants and Animals, Anatomy and Physiology of, Structure and Function in

The close relationship between the anatomy of plants and animals and their respective physiologies gives plants and animals their identifying characteristics. Scripture gives us little information about the structure of God other than God is a spirit (Genesis 1:2), but Scripture clearly points out the three distinct persons of God (Matthew 3:16–17). Comment on the three persons of God and the role and function attributed to each person. (8.2.1.2)

• Research the structure of a flower. Dissect a similar flower into its basic parts. Identify each part of the flower, and write two or three sentences explaining the function of each structure. Research the books of John and Matthew from the Bible, and identify the function for each person in the Godhead.
• Make a chart of the human digestive system. Then identify the function of each part of the system. Which part or parts of the system breaks down fats, which breaks down carbohydrates, and which breaks down proteins? Explain physical structure and physiology. How are they similar? How are they different? Make a chart to compare the work attributed to each person in the Trinity.

Organization of Cells, Tissues, Organs, Systems, and Organisms, Levels of

The organization of the human body is intricate and well-balanced because God has designed it. With all of humanity's knowledge and science, we have not yet unraveled all of its mysteries. However, God's relationship with us and His plan for

• Trace the flow of blood through the human circulatory system beginning with its entry into the right atrium of the heart. Be sure to include the chambers of the heart, the types of blood vessels, valves, and the relationship that the circulatory

our salvation is as simple as His love for us (John 3:16). Instill confidence in your students that God's salvation is a free gift of His love. (8.2.1.3)

system has with the respiratory system. Review 1 Corinthians 12:4–11. Compare how the body's parts work together with the body of Christ, which also works together. For what purpose do the people of God work together? See 1 Corinthians 12:7.

• Compare and contrast the cells of the blood in regards to number, size, and shape. What purpose does each cell provide? Explain how these cells work together. Then, explain the path these cells follow in the hierarchy of becoming tissue, organs, and an organ system. Read Psalm 16, and compare the path our blood takes to the path of life God speaks to us about in Psalm 16:11.

Photosynthesis and Cellular Respiration

Photosynthesis is a perfect example of God's continued care for us. He provides us, through the food manufactured by plants, all of the energy we need to run our bodies. Through the sun and plants, we get our food and oxygen. God gives us our spiritual energy through the Holy Spirit. The Holy Spirit keeps us close to the Lord. As we take in Christ, God replaces our sin with forgiveness and eternal life through Jesus Christ, just as cellular respiration replaces harmful carbon dioxide with life-sustaining oxygen (Genesis 1:29–31; Romans 5:18–21). (8.2.1.4)

• Research photosynthesis, and identify the energy source that makes photosynthesis work. Detail in sequence the steps involved in photosynthesis. What are the raw materials that plants need to engage in photosynthesis? What energy do plants get from photosynthesis? What energy is passed on to animals through photosynthesis? What are the by-products of photosynthesis? Read Colossians 1:24–28. Identify the energy of which Paul speaks. How is that energy active in us today?

• Make a teaching diagram of cellular respiration. In the diagram, include the exchange of products and the energy that is used. Be sure to write detailed specifics that tell the reader each step of the process. Identify which harmful substances are released during the process and what replaces these harmful substances. Read 2 Corinthians 8:9. Describe the great exchange Jesus performed for us. What did Jesus take from us? What did He give to us? Present this exchange on a poster.

• Read 2 Samuel 22, and identify the source of human survival. Write several paragraphs making an analogy between the sun as the source of energy for all life processes and God as the source of all life processes.

Plant and Animal Cells, Nucleus of

As the nucleus of a plant or animal cell directs the activities of those cells, the Bible tells us that God directs all of our activities, providing us with all that we need (Psalm 145:15–16), especially the forgiveness, new life, and salvation that is ours in Christ Jesus (Acts 4:12). Help students to see Jesus Christ as the nucleus of Christianity. (8.2.1.5)

• On an 8½ × 11 piece of paper, draw a plant cell, emphasizing the nucleus. Identify each part of the nucleus, and explain the function of each part of the nucleus in sustaining life. Prepare an oral presentation that explains how the nucleus of a plant cell directs all the life processes of the plant. Read Psalm 145:15–16, and describe how God is

the nucleus of our lives.
• Write a detailed explanation of the parts of an animal cell and its nucleus. Explain how the nucleus of an animal cell contains the information necessary to carry out life functions. Read John 14:6 and Isaiah 48:17, and tell where all who are saved find the source of and direction for their new and eternal life.

Photosynthesis, Process of

As green plants are the producers set forth by God as a means of transferring the sun's energy to food, God sent His Son to bring the energy essential for eternal life. See John 8:12. But because of sin, people naturally avoid and reject that light (John 3:19–21). Encourage students to reflect on how God has moved us from the darkness of sin into the light of salvation. (8.2.1.6)

• During the course of a seven-day week, make a list of all you needed to survive. Then, make a list of everything you would want to take with you on a seven-day camping trip. Cross off anything that is absolutely not necessary for your survival. After you have finished, review the steps that plants go through for their survival. How do they turn sunlight into food energy? Read Hebrews 12:1–3, and reflect on what needs to be crossed off so that we can more easily walk in the light.
• Research photosynthesis and write a detailed 300–500 word report explaining how plants use sunlight, water, and carbon dioxide to make and store sugar. Then, read Matthew 4:12–17; Luke 2:30–32; and John 8:12, and reflect on how Jesus' light provides us with all that we need to obtain eternal life.

Organisms, Nutrition and Energy of

Organisms take in nutrients in different manners, but one thing is consistent: all organisms need energy to survive. Scripture tells us that we need God's energy both to survive in physical form and to achieve eternal life (John 4:13; 6:32–35). As you teach this lesson, help students to realize what scriptural nutrients are needed to sustain eternal life. (8.2.1.7)

• Explain how herbivores, including human vegetarians, get the nutrients needed for life processes. List some plants that provide sugars or carbohydrates, plants that provide proteins, and plants that provide fats. Then explain how this plant energy is transferred to secondary consumers. Read Psalm 145:15–16 and John 6:56–58, and reflect on how God has given us elements that not only support our internal structures but also nourish us for eternal life.
• Compare the digestive systems of an amoeba, an earthworm, and a human being. Which system is the most complex, and what is the least complex? Explain how each system works and the main source of food energy. How is waste material eliminated? Read Matthew 15:10–19, and explain this teaching of Jesus in which He makes reference to the digestive system. To which commandments does Jesus refer in verse 19?

63

Cells, Animal, Structures and Functions of

Cells are magnificent creations of God. Some animals are made up on one cell; others have many. But left alone or when combined with others cells, they carry on life functions. Somewhat similarly, each verse of the Bible carries the essence of eternal life. When combined, they form the chapters and books of God's revealed Word. Scripture tells us that God's plan for salvation has been going on from Adam and Eve to Abraham and Noah, from Moses to David, and from John the Baptist to Jesus (Genesis, Exodus, Leviticus, 1 Samuel, and Luke). Each played a significant part of God's plan. Relate each verse of the Bible as the cell that provides us with some aspect of the truth that leads to eternal salvation. (8.2.1.8)

• Pretend to be a tour guide. You have devised a miniaturization process that is capable of shrinking your clients to microscopic size, and you have a ship that is capable of penetrating the pores of an animal cell's membrane. On a sheet of paper, write the tour presentation that you would make to the tourists. Make sure that you cover the cell membrane, cytoplasm, vacuoles, nucleus, chromosomes, and mitochondria. Explain each part of the cell by describing its physical structure and its process. Comment on the wondrous design of God, the Creator who enabled tiny cells to be able to do so much.
• After researching the structures of an animal cell, create a PowerPoint presentation that shows each structure and the function it provides. Include in the presentation the following animal cell structures: cell membrane, cytoplasm, vacuoles, chromosomes, mitochondria, and cell nucleus. Sometimes those who meet within Christian congregations for small-group Bible study are referred to as a cell or a cell group. Relate this kind of cell to the structure and function of an animal cell. See Romans 12:4–5.

Cells, Plant, Structures and Functions of

Each cell of every living thing is a tiny community of its own as well as part of the larger community of the whole organism. How like the local church and the Church universal this is! Every person has a unique combination of talents and abilities and is given a new identity and purpose at Baptism (1 Corinthians 12:13). We live out our connection with other believers in a local congregation where we are in an intimate community. All the cells, local churches, of the Church universal act out the Lord's master plan, often without even realizing how it affects the whole. In the final test on this unit, you may be asked what each structure of the cell contributes. Your question to yourself after that might be: what contribution do you make within the Christian community? (8.2.1.9)

• Draw what humans might look like if God made our cells with cell walls—no other variables change, just cell walls. Explain your drawing in writing. After seeing the variety of creations posted in the classroom, have groups evaluate God's design of human cells with only a membrane.
• Set up small groups to be each part of the cell. Challenge them to dress the part! Let each small group speak in turn to a panel of judges to convince them that their part is most important to the cell. Judges then decide which group was the most convincing. Review 1 Corinthians 12:12–27.

Mitosis and Cell Differentiation

Only living cells can produce more living cells. This is a key concept that needs to be stressed. Evolutionists believe that living cells suddenly sprang forth from nonliving cells. They say we all came from nonliving ooze. The newest theory says

• Cells differ in size, shape, and function. In people, white blood cells have more lysosomes. Red blood cells have more mitochondria and vacuoles. Nerve cells have a significantly different size and shape as well as more mitochondria. In plants, stomata cells

we came from viruses. To debunk this popular assumption, start with this very standard—mitosis occurs only in living cells! God's progression of creation started with energy, then nonliving water and minerals, and finally living beings. Even evolutionists do not refute the progression which was written out when the Bible was recorded. (8.2.1.10)

differ in shape from a root hair cell. Work in groups to compare and contrast a list of animal and plant cells using Web sites such as www.cellsalive.com and schooldiscovery.com and search for "electron microscope." You may also choose to Google individual cells by name. Marvel at the incredible diversity even in these brief samples. Create a visual praise wall of the drawings of cell diversity in the church lobby. As a class, decide on the title.

• Where does human life begin? In your study of cell mitosis, you might branch into the current political debate over stem cell research. What does a headline like "What is the value of a clump of cells—another human or a new hope for the diseased and dying?" Notice the connotation of "clump of cells" and "hope" as you discuss bias in reporting. Since Lutherans do not believe the end justifies the means (Romans 3:8), we favor using adult stem cells to fight disease rather than using embryonic stem cells. In addition, we believe a person begins at conception (Psalm 51:5 implies a soul at conception). In our technological age, the question is often not can we but should we? The slippery slope of humans determining life and death choices is what many Christians fear. Report on this controversy.

Organisms, Structure and Organization of

In first-century Palestine, Jesus said, "Even the very hairs on your head are all numbered" (Matthew 10:30 NIV). People then were amazed. Now we know the best estimate for the number of cells in a human body is fifty million million. (No, that's not a typo!) Visualize for your students how much that number represents. Ask them if God even knows how many cells they have? (Yes, He does!) What does this suggest about God? (8.2.1.11)

• If you asked for a specific book at your local library's reference desk, finding that title is now fairly simple even though the library may need to request it from a distant city. What organization is used? (A specific book number code is used that tells what shelf section it would be on in which library of the state's library system) Name and describe other organizational systems. (NBA sports, taxonomies, government structures) What do organizational structures help us do? (Define relationships.) What is the organizational structure of your church, and where do you and the other students fit in it?

• When viewed holistically, the individual cell in the circulatory system or the skeletal system looks rather minor, even expendable. Not so from God's point of view. Had either you or one of your classmates been the only human alive, Jesus would have died to save you because God counts each person as that valuable. There are no expendable people. Today's science community sometimes sees cell systems objectively, which leads them to make value decisions about stem cells as well as premature organ donation and assisted suicide. Parts make up the whole, but the whole is actually greater than the parts.

Organs and Organ Systems

There are times as teachers when we may feel that our job is unimportant. Always remember that God has called you to where you are—connecting with, serving, and relating to each student in your class. He is using you and your colleagues for His kingdom! Stress to your students that each one is a unique and important part of the class, just as each organ and system is important for the functioning of the body. (8.2.1.12)

• Evolutionists have difficulty explaining how random accidents could produce something as complex as the eye. Take time to study the function of each part of the human eye. Explain how each part is necessary in order to see.
• Just as there are many important parts to making a school or class work correctly, so it is with our bodies. Use 1 Corinthians 12 as a starting point for writing a devotion based on the concept "One body; many parts."

Flowering Plants, Parts of

Those who suffer from hay fever or other allergies may not always appreciate pollen. However, pollen is vital for the survival of a flowering plant. Remind students that they pollinate others through their actions and words. The Holy Spirit uses us to spread the Word to others and perpetuate the Christian species. (8.2.1.13)

• After studying fruit-bearing plants, read Galatians 5:22, and come up with ways you can reflect the fruit of the Spirit in your life and relationships.
• Work with your classmates to design and construct a bulletin board for your classroom. Have one classmate design a vine with leaves out of green construction paper. Have other students each draw and cut out a piece of fruit. Label each fruit with one of the results of the Spirit at work, which are listed in Galatians 5:22.
• Bring in a flowering plant still in its budding stage. Do not tell the other students what kind of plant it is. Invite classmates to analyze the leaf and bud structure of the plant to try to identify it. Once the plant flowers, have classmates reveal their guesses. Outward appearances can be deceiving. Just as some people may give all the appearances of being a Christian, they might not believe in their heart. Read and reflect on Jesus' description of hypocrites recorded in Matthew 23:27–28. Identify and describe times when you have been guilty of hypocrisy.

Proteins, Carbohydrates, and Fats

As a teacher, you provide the building materials for your students to learn. Thanks be to God that through Christ Jesus we are rebuilt into new creations (2 Corinthians 5:17). As you teach this standard, remind your students of the building materials of faith; the means of grace and Word and Sacraments. (8.2.1.14)

• For the period of a week, record everything you drink and eat. At the end of the week, analyze your diet. Do you have a healthy diet, or do you need to rethink your choices? It is said that we "are what we eat." This concept is true in our spiritual lives as well. Record for a week what TV shows, movies, Internet sites, and video games you see and what songs you hear. Analyze these choices. Is your spiritual diet healthy, or are you building with the wrong materials?
• After studying the building blocks of living

organisms, study 1 Thessalonians 5:11 and brainstorm ways you can build each other up in Christ.

Toxic Substances, Effects of

Sometimes our relationships with parents, teachers, or even students can end up toxic. Reflect on your relationships. Are you building them on Christ and His forgiveness? Pray for proper perspective and a humble heart as you lead your students to the feet of Jesus today. Remind students daily of God's great love for them and that He sent Jesus to die in our place. Pay special attention to toxic attitudes in your class, and seek ways to model for your students a more Christlike love for each other. (8.2.1.15)

• Identify some of the chemicals stored right now in your home. Tell how these chemicals are used. Read and reflect on the meaning of Malachi 3:2–4 (e.g., sometimes we face harsh situations, but God cleans and purifies us as we go through bad situations).
• One fascinating concept in chemistry is that of acids and bases. A strong acid combined in exact proportions with a strong base will yield neutrality. Explain the reaction that takes place when hydrochloric acid (HCl) is combined with lye (sodium hydroxide—$NaOH$). On their own, these two chemicals will severely injure a person. However, when combined, the two yield salt water ($NaCl$—table salt—and H_2O). Write the chemical formula to describe this combination and reaction. Use this model to show that with God even the impossible is possible. Those who seem powerful and caustic can be neutralized through the mighty power of God's Word.

8.2.2   Ecosystems

Food Webs, Global, Ocean, and Land

Scripture tells us that God created all of the natural resources of this world (Genesis 1:1–25) and placed humans in charge of those resources (Genesis 1:26). God spoke of the resources as being good. As stewards of God's creation, it is necessary to instill in future generations the knowledge and understanding to wisely manage the Earth's natural resources. Help raise students' awareness that the responsibility for the planet's health and future will one day be in their hands. (8.2.2.1)

• Using the Internet or another resource, construct a list of biomes that make up the biosphere of planet Earth. Next, choose a land biome and a water biome. Identify thirty plants and animals for each of the biomes. Put the organisms in each biome into an interactive food web to show the interlocking relationships among the organisms. Read Genesis 1:1–25, and identify on what day of creation each of the organisms in your two biomes was created.
• Research the different land and water biomes of planet Earth. Construct three different food chains from each biome, and write a paragraph explaining what might happen to the global biosphere if the creatures in the food chains were to become extinct. When God created people, He gave them the specific responsibility to manage creation's resources (Genesis 1:27–28). Write a personal letter to God recounting how humankind has managed creation's resources since the time of Adam and Eve.

Matter, Transformation of, between Environments and Organisms

Not only did God create all of the resources for humanity (Genesis 1:1–25), He continually replenishes them through natural cycles. This replenishment is important to the continued well-being of humanity. Over the years, many wars have been fought over control of natural resources. Read Matthew 9:1–8. Discuss Jesus' concern for both physical and spiritual human needs. What other examples can students give of how our Savior provided people with blessings for both physical well-being and spiritual well-being? (8.2.2.2)

• Research and draw a model of the water cycle, oxygen and carbon cycle, and nitrogen cycle. Draw the models on notebook paper. Label each part of each cycle. Then, using a piece of poster board, make a display of the three cycles. Write a paragraph explaining how matter is transformed and thereby replenishes needed natural resources. Read Mark 2:1–12, and make an analogy between how God continually provides for us through natural cycles and how He continually makes us well by forgiving our sins.

• Research the relationship between respiration and photosynthesis. Draw a chart explaining the process, and prepare and deliver a three-minute oral presentation on the topic. Be prepared to answer how plants prepare oxygen and what they need to complete the process. Explain how the plants give off oxygen as a by-product. Read Matthew 26:26–29, and write a paragraph comparing and contrasting God's continual wiping away of our sins with the replenishment of life-sustaining oxygen.

Environmental Change through Natural Processes

God created the world so that it was good (Genesis 1) and in perfect harmony. After the fall, sin led to corruption that has caused much human suffering, both spiritually and physically. Great empires, such as the Roman Empire, fell because of internal changes and corruption, but natural disasters such as the volcanic eruption of Pompeii led to swift desolation. Even with all of our current knowledge and power, it is insignificant when compared to God's power and climatic or geological events. Stress the importance of seeking God's continual blessing and forgiveness (1 John 1:8–9). (8.2.2.3)

• Research the destruction of Pompeii, and write a 300–500-word report on the type of volcano that destroyed Pompeii and how it affected the local environment. Next, research the eruption of Mount St. Helens. Write down some facts on how powerful the eruption was and how the eruption affected the global community. After making your comparison, read Genesis 7 and relate how sin's destructive power relates to Earth's geological events.

• Research global warming and explain how the greenhouse effect has the potential of drastically changing the Earth's climate. Write your hypothesis of what would happen if the Earth's polar caps completely melted. How would it change the global community and, more specifically, your own community? Read Jeremiah 14, and write three to five paragraphs contrasting how a global drought might affect people and nations. What ultimate purpose does God desire through all the events of human history? See 1 Timothy 2:3–4.

Ecosystems and Overpopulation

From what we can observe, ecosystems generally live in balance if left alone. For Darwin's theory of gradual evolution to work, there must be overpopulation so that only the fittest survive. So overpopulation is seen as a good thing. For Gould's theory of punctuated equilibrium, the newest evolutionary theory, there must be a sparse population so that only the fittest survive. Gould says that balance is lost when a catastrophic event occurs. Only those that can adapt to the more rigorous requirements survive. Eventually a boom of certain higher organisms occurs with the need for another catastrophic event to repeat the improved species cycle. So underpopulation is a good thing. Humans don't seem to fit either population theory. World wars created catastrophic population events, but did only the fittest survive? Western educated parents use birth control to reduce population growth artificially so overpopulation and survival fitness do not come into play. As humans bring foreign plants that have no natural enemies to an area, they can overpopulate, rapidly changing an ecosystem in dramatic ways. Invariably, the end result is too often the extinction of species, which reduces the possibility for evolution. This standard focuses attention exclusively on Darwinian evolution. Have students spot the bias in their textbooks. (8.2.2.4)

• Because of tremendous human overpopulation in China, the government dictated a one child policy. The result was an increase in female baby infanticide as well as female fetal abortion. Does intentional gender specific infant death occur in nature anywhere? Why does it occur in humans? (sin) What does this imply? (Use logical deduction to postulate. Humans are radically different from animals, some humans manipulate events because of self-interest, "surplus people" are devalued in some societies, and so on.)

• Challenge small groups to develop a set of instructions for creating a small, ecologically balanced ecosystem. It must include climate, soil conditions, plants, and animals. Once you have a system designed, ask how much effort and thought this required? How much attention would it require per day? Per week? Per month? Is it self-sustaining? Next, introduce a family of four into the ecosystem. How much effort or thought is now required? How much attention? This is the world God sustains with His almighty power.

Symbiotic Relationships (e.g., Predator and Prey, Parasitism, Mutualism, and Commensalisms)

One of the greatest joys of teaching is to see students mature in their faith. This maturation is evidenced in their dealings with classmates. As you teach this standard, encourage your students to find ways to help each other. If your class is large, you may organize a secret angel project. Have students draw a name and then write anonymous notes of encouragement to that student for a period of time. (8.2.2.5)

• In Acts 6 and 7, we read of a man named Stephen, who was called to serve food to widows. Eventually, through the Holy Spirit, Stephen gave bold testimony about the Lord. Analyze the Early Church in Acts 1–8, looking for the relationships mentioned and the symbiosis of the Church.

• Research a specific parasite, and present your findings to the class. While parasitism usually harms an organism, the parasite could not survive without the host. As disgusting as it may sound, that is actually quite similar to our relationship to God! Our sin caused Jesus to die on the cross, yet we could not live without God.

Environmental Changes, Gradual and Sudden

Have you faced a flood recently? Maybe you have had a litany of phone calls, complaints, papers to grade, or other distractions. Remember God's word in Psalm 46:10. Remind your students that faith in Christ causes a change. It changes us (Romans 8:1–8). Sometimes changes happen gradually; at other times, the change is sudden. But regardless of how it happens, God's power does indeed change us into the people He would have us become. (8.2.2.6)

• In a way, the changes that take place in our world resemble the changes that take place in the lives of maturing Christians. Some experience instant dramatic changes that alter their life forever, such as Paul experienced, while others may experience changes in their lives that gradually bring them close to Christ. Describe the kind of change the power of God brought into your life when you became His follower.

• Contact the Institute for Creation Research (www.icr.org) for materials regarding the evidence of the flood in archaeology. Study and report on some aspect of environmental change. Other resources can be found through Jeremiah Films at www.jeremiahfilms.com.

8.2.3 Human Life

Body Systems, Functioning of, and Effects of Disease

The human body is one of the most complex of God's creations. The human body demonstrates many interdependent relationships to keep the body in a homeostatic condition. The skeletal system and the muscular system work in unison so that we may move about freely. In Jesus' prayer for all believers (John 17:20–26), He provides us with an interdependent view of the relationship between God the Father, the Creator; Jesus, the Redeemer; and believers. They are both God, one being in unison with the other, working to create and save us. As you teach this lesson, stress that Jesus is God. Teach that Jesus was sent by the Father for the fulfillment of His plan for the redemption of all people, and instill in students that, like two muscles working together for movement, God the Father and God the Son work as one, together with God the Spirit, to save us. (8.2.3.1)

• Using the Internet or another resource, make a list of the joints of the human skeletal system. Write a paragraph on each of the joints, telling how each specific joint allows a different type of motion that gives the human body its strength and agility. Read John 3:1–21, and use the human skeletal system to make an analogy to explain how God the Father, God the Son, and God the Holy Spirit work together to give us agility (truth) and strength (salvation).

• Research the three main types of muscles in the human body. Make a chart comparing the functions of the three different muscles. Identify the function and capabilities of each muscle type. Prepare an oral presentation explaining how the individual muscles work together in unison. Read Acts 2, and compare how God used imperfect humans, His disciples, working together by His power to spread the Word.

Pathogens and Body Functions

Scripture tells us that all of God's creation was good until the fall into sin in Genesis 1. Since the fall into sin, God has used pathogens to help remind us that He is the cure, both physically and spiritually (Luke 5:17–25). Students can easily relate to the pain and suffering of disease. As you teach about illnesses, help students recognize the relationship between the consequences of sin, such as a disease (Matthew 8:5–17) that affects the

• Research which pathogens cause tetanus, measles, and athlete's foot. Write several paragraphs explaining how each disease develops, spreads, and is treated. Then, identify how our body responds to each of the pathogens and what types of medication might be given to treat the diseases caused by these pathogens. Read Luke 13:1–8, and explain the relationship between the harmful effects of disease and the sin that plagues us all.

physical nature, and sin that affects the soul. Our gracious and mighty Lord demonstrates His power over both. (8.2.3.2)

• Research AIDS, and identify the type of pathogens that causes the disease. Write a 300–500-word report on the life span of the disease, its treatment, and its effects on a person. Be sure to include physical effects, emotional effects, and social effects. Compare the harmful effects of AIDS to humanity's fall into sin (Genesis 1), and hypothesize how sin without God's intervention through Jesus Christ would be like AIDS without a cure. Be prepared to defend your hypothesis against the questions of fellow classmates.

Parasites and Body Functions

As parasites interrupt the normal functions of the human body, so parasitic relationships exist between humans. We want to find our comfort and security in our sinful nature rather than in God's grace and forgiveness. God continually warns us that Satan, the world, and our own sinful nature will tempt us to follow the devil (Proverbs 1:8–19) but that we should not give in to those temptations. Our loving God provides His followers with the power to resist and withstand temptation (1 Corinthians 10:13). Point out that just as parasites can harm their hosts, harmful peer temptations and pressure can be physically and spiritually dangerous to human hosts who are unable to ward off their influence. (8.2.3.3)

• Construct a chart with columns. In the first, show how tapeworms, hookworms, and roundworms enter the human body. In a second column, list the parts of the human body that these parasites affect. In a third column, name the harmful effects that these parasites can cause the human body. In a fourth column, write the prescribed treatment for the listed parasites. In a fifth column, write a method for the prevention of the listed parasites. Read Proverbs 1:8–19, and think about how various temptations by others, including friends, can be as dangerous to us when they attach themselves to us as if they were parasites.
• Write a fictional story about a person infested with a tapeworm. In the story, teach the life cycle of the tapeworm, its harmful effects, and treatment possibilities. Provide the story with two separate conclusions, one with successful treatment and the second without treatment. Then, read Romans 6:15–23, and rewrite the story using peer temptations to smoke cigarettes in place of the tapeworm. Choose only one ending. Be prepared to read your story to the rest of the class.

Body, Defense System of

Did you ever wonder what white blood cells did before Adam and Eve sinned? Even after the fall, Scriptures record that some people lived to be as much as 969 years old. The Chinese understanding of wellness is that when the body is in healthy balance, it naturally fights off infection. Their healing goal is a more total health approach. Consider the total health of Adam and Eve's bodies, unexposed to the ravages of pollution, chemical by-products, animal and plant enzymes, UV

• Go online to research microbes. Google "cold virus + remedies" to learn of lab work currently underway to fend off viruses, some attacking the virus itself and some fortifying the body's defense mechanisms. Google "free radicals + antioxidants" to find a wealth of information on the body's defense systems. What a gift God has given us in these bodies we have! Label Band-Aids for younger grades with notations like "God's miracle: new skin!" or "God fixes booboos."

rays, and the like. Imagine their dismay when their temperature climbed to 102 degrees to kill bacteria or they watched the first scab form! Sin not only affected early human work habits, it affected even their bodies as it still does today. (8.2.3.4)

• Our souls also have defense systems. See Ephesians 6:10–18, which lists the armor God has told us to put on as our defense against the evil one. All Christians have access to this protection in what the Bible calls warfare against the spiritual forces of evil in the heavenly realms (v. 12). Make bulletin covers of this under the title "The Soul's Defense System."

Human Activities Producing Changes in the Natural Processes

Are Americans good for the planet—for the air, water, animal, and plant life? Research how the United States compares to other countries in its use of energy resources, specifically nonrenewable resources. What does a Christian witness really call us to do? It brings about a radical change in viewpoint! Why? Because Genesis 1:28 tells us God gave us dominion of the Earth, sharing in God's kingly rule. Every one of us was adopted into God's family. Princes and princesses have responsibilities for the kingdom and must often sacrifice accordingly. As good stewards of what has been entrusted to our care, including creation, we look to the day God says, "Well done, good and faithful servant" (Matthew 25:21). (8.2.3.5)

• Consider the water cycle, the carbon and oxygen cycle, and the nitrogen cycle. Point out that God doesn't waste anything. Phone an area business in charge of recycling. Ask for a representative to visit your school. Some have prepared videos and statistics specifically for the waste your school generates. Listen to suggestions for possible waste management projects. As a class, consider taking on one suggestion for six weeks. Keep records. After the time period, set up an interview with your local newspaper, and share what the class did.
• Environmental science usually involves discussion of moral values. Compare the development, preservation, and conservation viewpoints of manufacturing versus environmentalists. Weigh the costs (monetary, future availability, natural beauty, safety) to the benefits (economics, political power, convenience). How does being an eternal person affect your viewpoint?
• Habitat destruction plays a role in extinction, which in turn plays a role in medicine. Almost half the medicines sold today contain chemicals originally found in the wild. In 1854, Chief Seattle said, "Whatever befalls the Earth befalls the children of the Earth. We did not weave the web of life; we are merely a strand in it. Whatever we do to the web, we do to ourselves." One person may not think he or she makes much difference. Remember the parable of the talents. One got ten, one five, and one got one. Had the steward with one talent used it faithfully, would he have received the same praise as the others (Luke 19:1–27)?
• Lutheran World Relief (LWR), a charitable organization of The Lutheran Church—Missouri Synod (LCMS), works hard to help third-world countries find ways to dispose of waste safely to keep drinking water pure. You might visit their Web site for specific countries where their work is being done. Take one day of the year and donate your regular food costs to a specific LWR project.

Health Habits and Practices, Helpful and Harmful

As you probably remember from your education classes while in college, modeling is the most effective form of teaching. Students can quickly pick up on hypocrisy. If you are telling your students to lead a healthy life, it will mean a lot more to them if you are also living a healthy life. As you teach through this standard, analyze your own lifestyle. Also remind your students (and yourself) that even when we make poor decisions regarding our lives, we have forgiveness through Jesus (Romans 8:33). (8.2.3.6)

• Analyze the impact of sin in our environment today. As a starting point, use Romans 8:18–25.
• Develop a personal plan for increasing your physical fitness. After sharing your plan with your classmates, discuss the importance of spiritual fitness. Develop a plan for spiritual fitness (e.g. reading a chapter of the Bible each day, reading a devotion book each day).

8.2.4   Heredity

Chromosomes and Genetic Information

Genes provide the framework for our physical development, the road map that tells us who we will become—male or female, short or tall, slim or heavy, blue or green eyes. But they do not provide us with a road map for our spiritual salvation. While we inherited original sin from one man, Adam (Genesis 3), God gives us salvation through one man, Jesus Christ, God's Son. Read and reflect on Romans 5:17. (8.2.4.1)

• Make a genetic chart showing the possibility of a child being a boy or a girl. First, identify the chromosome that determines the sex of a human child and from which parent the chromosome comes. Then, show possible variations of male and female birth as you go through three generations. Read Proverbs 22:6, and reflect on the importance of parents in a child's natural growth and development.
• Using the Internet or another resource, identify a list of genes and the chromosomes on which they reside. Write three to four sentences about each gene and the characteristics they produce. Research the Human Genome Project, and write a report on what the possible outcome might be of such research. Read Genesis 5:1–32, and find the average life span of the individuals named. If during that time period, every person had similar life spans, how many children might a family raise? Why would longevity have been especially important during these early years of human history?

Traits and Genes

Scripture tells us that we are all descendants from the same set of parents, Adam and Eve (Genesis 3:20). We have inherited traits from our parents, and the variety of genes has been greatly multiplied because of the long lifespans of our first ancestors. Adam lived 930 years (Genesis 5:4), and Methuselah lived 969 years (Genesis 5:25–27). Point out that all of the traits we have come from our ancestors but that some of the genes we have are latent genes and spread on to others without being evident in us, just as God sometimes uses

• Using the Internet, research the chromosomes and genes associated with human sexual development. Identify which traits come from the male and which traits come from the female. Explain how latent genes are passed on without being active in the individual doing the passing. Identify several traits that we inherit from our parents. Read Genesis 5:4–5, 25–27, and reflect on why humans no longer live as long as our early ancestors. Why was there more need to have large families at the beginning of creation?

INFORMATION BY TOPIC

DISCUSSION POINTS/ACTIVITIES

non-Christians to spread His Word. Such an example would be the persecution of early Christians that spread them and their influence throughout the world. (8.2.4.2)

• Compare the life spans recorded in Genesis 5 with those recorded in Genesis 11. Speculate on the causes for the decrease in human longevity.
• Research genetic defects and identify the most common defects. What causes these defects, and are we able to treat them? For each defect identified, list the common characteristics associated with that defect. Assume that you have one of the defects. All health problems are consequences of the fall into sin. Write three to five paragraphs describing sin as the ultimate defect.

Reproduction, Asexual and Sexual

The Scriptures place great importance on the contributions that parents make in their offspring's development (Proverbs 22:6). While children physically receive half of their genes from their mother and half from their father, it is important to understand that these characteristics are physical. When it comes to behaviors, more focus should be on the training and care that children receive from the family. It is especially important to raise children in a nurturing environment, including discipline (Proverbs 23:13–14; 29:15–17) and teaching (Proverbs 3:1–6). Although original sin passes naturally from generation to generation, we can also tell our children of God's grace and forgiveness (Psalm 78:3–7). (8.2.4.3)

• Make a list of characteristics that you share with each of your parents. Include eye color, hair color, height, and other physical characteristics. Then, discuss with your parents what behaviors you exhibit that are similar to your parents' behavior when they were your age. Examine the results, and write two or three paragraphs explaining your conclusions. Read Proverbs 3–4, and make a list of good things that your parents have instilled in you.
• Talk with your grandparents if possible. If not, you can talk with your parents. Find out about your parents when they were children. Compare your parents' childhoods to yours. What did your parents do for fun? Did they have the same bedtime, chores, and expectations that are imposed upon you? Read Proverbs 22:6, and reflect on the things your parents have taught you about Jesus and His love.

Traits and Skills, Acquired

Christians acquire similar traits once they take on righteousness through faith in Jesus Christ (Isaiah 61:10). But even Christians do not possess the abilities or skills necessary to achieve eternal life on our own (John 14:6; Romans 5:19; and John 11:25–26). Point out that we acquire sin from our first parents' original fall into sin, but we all acquire redemption from God. God gives His Holy Spirit to His children so that we may serve God and others with the skills for Christian living He has given us (Luke 11:11–13). (8.2.4.4)

• Write a definition of an acquired trait and a definition of an acquired skill. Take a sheet of paper, and divide it into two columns. On the left side, make a list of acquired traits, and on the right side, make a list of acquired skills. Draw a line connecting skills that might develop from acquired traits. Then, write a paragraph explaining your reasoning. Read Isaiah 61:10, and think about what traits you acquired from God through the merits of Christ Jesus.
• Write up a list of acquired traits, and divide them into positive traits and negative traits. Investigate what factors link acquired traits to an individual. Hypothesize how to prevent acquiring negative traits (John 8:31–32). Read John 14:6; Romans 5:19; and John 11:25–26, and identify the common ability that God has given us in order to ensure our salvation.

Reproduction, Asexual

Scripture tells us that we are all exactly alike in one drastic characteristic: sin (Romans 3:21–23). In the same manner, we all share in God's plan for redemption (Romans 3:24–26; John 3:16). Throughout Scripture, God gives us many examples that show we are all the same in His eyes (John 17:2; Acts 17:30; 2:17). Sin brings the same destructive consequences to each human life. But God in Christ has provided a cure for sin, and He desires all people to receive it (1 Timothy 2:3–4). (8.2.4.5)

• Research the two forms of asexual reproduction called budding and regeneration. Draw a model explaining each. Be sure to label each model correctly, and demonstrate that each offspring will be exactly like the parent organism. Read Romans 3:21–23, and reflect on how we are alike in sin before God's eyes. Only after we put on His cloak of righteousness are we changed from nonbelievers to believers.

• Generate a list of organisms that reproduce asexually. Make a list of as many characteristics as you can about each of the organisms, and then compare the anatomy of each organism. Do any of the organisms contain a sophisticated nervous system, digestive system, or circulatory system? What does the simplicity of these organisms tell you about the limitations of asexual organisms? How are humans different? See Genesis 1:26–27.

• Read Galatians 3:26–29, and reflect on the commonality Christians enjoy. We are all one in the Lord.

Reproduction, Sexual, and Combination of Traits

Put up a bulletin board titled "Designer Genes." How long ago did God work out the exact combination in your students' parents' reproductive cells to make them (Ephesians 1:4)? (8.2.4.6)

• Combine math and science in this lesson as you apply exponentials to the possibilities of a specific individual's biology. There are 20,000 to 25,000 genes in a single human DNA strand. Using permutations, how many possible combinations are there? God says we are not any combination of traits, but are formed individually, deliberately (Psalm 139:13). God has predetermined the length of our days (Psalm 139:16). Thus, it is God who controls our survival and not the chance presence of traits facilitating survival.

• Include mutations, genetic aberrations in sexual reproduction's combinations of genetic codes, in the discussion of sexual reproduction. What is the difference between a mutation and a possible combination of chromosomes? (Mutations involve gene changes brought on by chemical means or radiation.) What is typically the result of a mutation? (99 percent are harmful or neutral in effect. Natural selection then eliminates mutations by immediate or early death or sterility.) Evolution rests on the principle of beneficial mutations genetically passed on in sexual reproduction. Evolutionists often point to the development of the nectarine, seedless oranges, and the Ancon breed of short-legged sheep. It is significant to note that in the above cases (1) oranges were not turned into carrots, and (2) someone manipulated the sexual cross in the sheep rather than random chance. By studying mutations here, we can begin to understand the huge leap of faith required by those who believe our world came to be without God's hand. Trace each person's hand, and write on it, "I am not the result of mutations!"

Organisms, Structure, Behavior, and Physiology of, and Variations in

Herein lies the difference between natural selection (microevolution) and Darwin's evolution in action, which results in a new species (macroevolution). Natural selection accounts for changes like those encountered by the famous Farmer Jones in the early 1920s. Farmer Jones sprayed DDT in his cow barn and killed off hundreds of thousands of flies, all but about ten. Three weeks later, because he left the door open, millions were back. He sprayed again. This time all but one hundred died. The cycle repeated for about four months, after which time the DDT didn't work anymore. What happened? Here's another example: due to climate change, vegetation changed and produced hard, dry seeds. Finches with hard beaks—rather than the previous majority with softer beaks—survived, producing a majority of hard-beaked finches. The final example is this: in 1848 Britain, the peppered moth was black and white speckled, a good camouflage for the local tree bark. Toward the end of that century, the rise of industrialism caused the lichens and trees to be covered with soot. It was noted that most peppered moths were now solid black. In each case, survival favored one variation over another of a specific species that lived to pass its genetic code to offspring. But did the genes change, or was the variation always there? God's people believe in natural selection, something dog breeders, plant breeders, and so on use to modify a specific animal or plant. But can a dog breeder breed for a winged dog or a plant breeder breed for a walking plant? Macroevolutionists would say that given enough time, yes, they could. God's people would say no. (8.2.4.7)

• Google "natural selection," and print off some of the studies. Make posters with the title "God Built in Variety. Why?" Put your thoughts on sticky notes, and attach them to the border of the display. What does variety tell us about God?
• Invite someone involved in the breeding of plants or animals into your classroom, specifically one who is breeding for a particular trait like a hybrid corn breeder or a person working for the orchid society. If there is no one locally, do a phone interview using a speaker phone. Prewrite questions. After the interview, move into higher level thinking by asking: What are the benefits and dangers of selective breeding? The benefits are larger, tastier food; more environmentally adapted seeds; and easier shipping of firmer fruit. The dangers are less flexibility if the environment changes, and the human decision making that determines the value of what to breed. To explore the negative repercussions, interview someone from the international seed bank. Go to www.rbgkew.org/uk/msbp/. Debate the pros and cons of this. Where does the God-given role of subduing the Earth (Genesis 1:28) come in, and where do we step over the line?

Reproduction, Sexual

Have you had one yet? One of those perfect students? Maybe the student isn't perfect in every way, but you may have had a student who almost always seemed to do the right thing. Maybe you have found yourself saying, "I wish I had a whole class of _____s." (Fill in the blank with the name of your perfect student.) Of course, we know that students are rarely alike. Those of us who have taught sibling combinations know this! Celebrate the differences God has given you to enjoy among your students. Thank God for the unique talents, abilities, and interests of each. (8.2.4.8)

• Identify the characteristics that you share with your mom and the ones you share with your dad. (Note: Assess the sensitivities among the students in your class before you decide to do this activity.) Once you have analyzed your list, discuss why God would choose for organisms—humans included—to have unique offspring.
• Research cloning. Discuss the ethical questions regarding cloning as well as the spiritual implications. Would cloned people be unique individuals with an individual soul? (Yes, they would!)

Breeding, Selective

The great thing about school is that each day is like a new creation. Students with very poor attitudes can have a change of heart the next day. Remind students that we are all new creations through faith in Jesus Christ (2 Corinthians 5:17). (8.2.4.9)

• Research a genetically engineered organism (e.g. beefalo, liger, etc.), and report to the class. From a biblical perspective, debate the ethics of breeding these plants and animals (e.g., is man playing God by breeding these plants and animals?).
• Investigate the history of eugenics and selective breeding in the twentieth century. How does God's command of stewardship along with the command to "be fruitful and multiply" (Genesis 1:28) guide us in our scientific decisions? What light does 1 Corinthians 6:12 shed on the topic?

8.2.5   Life in the Past

Adaptations

Scripture tells us that the fall into sin brought Adam and Eve the knowledge of good and evil they sought (Genesis 3). With their newfound knowledge of good and evil, the world also changed. Thorns and thistles and other adaptations by plants and behavioral adaptations by animals ensured that some would exist and others would die out. Those creatures that readily adapted had a better chance of survival. The great flood in Genesis 7 further complicated survival for animal and plant species, again because of human sin. Stress that God made the adaptation in order to effect human salvation. He sent His only Son as a human to keep the Law for us and to pay the penalty we deserved because of our sin. (8.2.5.1)

• Select two different species of animals, one that is still surviving and one that is extinct. Make a list of the behaviors of each species that either led to its adaptation and continued survival or its extinction. Examine how the Earth is changing—global warming, ozone depletion—and make a list of behaviors that people must assume if we are not to be threatened by our current behaviors. Thank God for the ability to adapt. God has given this to us because we are the crown of His creation.
• Research global warming and the melting of the ice caps and glaciers on Earth. How would the Earth change, and what adaptations would animals and people need to make in order to survive if the worst predictions come true? What behavioral changes must people make in order to reverse the melting of the ice caps, or is the process a natural part of the changing climate of

our planet and a result of original sin? Write several paragraphs in support of or against the fact that global warming is only being speeded up by our current behavior. Or write several paragraphs supporting a reversal of global warming if people change their harmful behaviors. Read Revelation 18, and reflect on sin's destructive nature.

Extinction

Scripture tells us that all of God's creation was good in Genesis 1–2 and that conditions began to change after Adam and Eve's fall into sin (Genesis 3). Before the fall, Adam and Eve walked naked upon the Earth without need for taking the lives of animals for covering. After the fall, death became a reality for plants, animals, and people both as individuals and as groups. Point out that extinction is part of the natural process in a sinful world. (8.2.5.2)

• Using the Internet or another resource, make a list of twenty-five species of animals and plants that have become extinct in the last one hundred years. Identify the main cause for each animal's extinction and write a report on factors involved in extinction. In the report, include the percentage of organisms that have become extinct because of human influence. Read Genesis 1:26 and 2:15. What does God expect of people with respect to His creatures?

• Consider that while you were sleeping last night, a force suddenly transported you onto an island filled with wild beasts, serpents, and an abundance of trees, grasses, and freshwater streams. On this island, you discovered five other eighth graders had also been transported so that there were three males and three females. You have no tools and are wearing only your nightclothes. Make a list of adaptations that you must undergo if you and your offspring are to survive. Write a story about your experience and include whether or not you would survive. Review the First Article of the Apostles' Creed and its explanation. What does this confession teach us about our ability to adapt?

Evolution, Theory of, and Diversity

Scripture provides us with a simple explanation for the diversity of living species on Earth. On the third day, He created vegetations and trees of all kinds (Genesis 1:11–13). God created creatures of the seas and birds of the air on the fifth day (Genesis 1:20–23). On the sixth day, God created animals of the land and man (Genesis 1:24–31). After each creation, God claimed that creation to be good and to multiply. To this day, many of God's creation have learned to adapt to a changing environment and populate the Earth. Others have failed to adapt and are now extinct. Stress that God is the Creator of all species on Earth and that no scientific evidence exists that any completely

• Make a chart listing the five kingdoms: Plantae, Animalia, Protista, Monera, and Fungi. Next, rank the kingdoms according to complexity of anatomic structure. Then, identify five species that would fall under each kingdom. Read Genesis 1:11–31, and identify the day on which each of the species was created.

• Choose a specific type of elephant, mountain lion, python, shark, hawk, and oak tree. Identify the genus and species for each organism you have selected. Next, identify each family from which your species is classified. Then, identify each order from which your species is classified. Repeat the process and identify the class, phylum, and kingdom. Read Genesis 2:8–15, and identify the general area of the garden of Eden.

new species has evolved from a species created by God. (8.2.5.3)

Identify several species of animals that live in that area today. What job has God given humanity through Adam? What responsibility do we have today for God's creatures?

Species, Diversity of

Evolution scientists who believe in Darwin's theory use the word *gradual* to debate with those of the Gould punctuated equilibrium group. The creationists have added their newest argument against both by advances in molecular biology, specifically protein formation. After water, our bodies are mostly made of various proteins. Proteins, in turn, are made of long chains of amino acids. There is a minimum of two hundred. The twenty-one different amino acids combine and fold or twist to determine a specific protein. Every cell depends on these different proteins. We now know that every amino acid must be present at the same moment to make specific proteins. They cannot gradually develop. Thus, Darwin's evolution as a theory has met a significant obstacle. And for this reason, the newest theory of punctuated equilibrium uses the idea of sudden leaps in the evolutionary process. These are due to cataclysms, which produce a huge number of mutations, a few of which survive and have all the necessary proteins at hand. It is important for students to hear that this standard, which informs your student texts, is currently being challenged. Christians declare in the Apostles' Creed each Sunday, "I believe in God the Father, Maker of heaven and Earth." Do we really believe what we recite? (8.2.5.4)

• Historically, people believed that maggots came from raw meat, that live animals came from decaying matter. They called this spontaneous generation. In 1668, Redi and then later Pasteur disproved this theory. With the microscope, scientists learned that life does not come from nonliving things. However, Darwin's gradual evolution theory must prove that life actually can spontaneously generate from chemicals since they presume a universe of gases and nonliving matter. In 1953, Stanley Miller passed a spark through a mixture of methane, hydrocarbons, water, and ammonia. He got some polypeptides, chemical chains similar in complexity to gelatin. Since then, others have experimented with chemicals using UV light and mild heating. The theory was that these polypeptides were supposed to stew in the primordial oceans and become more complex over millions of years. This was hailed as proof that life from nonlife was possible. However, chemists soon refuted this research with the fact that chemicals degrade over time rather than becoming more complex. This line of research reached a dead end since the possibility of polypeptides becoming living cells is as probable as throwing bowls of Jell-O into a warm ocean and produce living creatures! Why is it important to know about the gaps in evolutionary theory? A Godless universe is a lie, a lie increasingly accepted by intelligent people who assume science is always correct.

• Scientists who believe that diversity comes from gradual processes must answer this question: where are the transitional fossils? If a lizard develops into a bird, where is the creature that is 75% lizard 25% bird, then half lizard and half bird, then 25% lizard and 75% bird? To date, no transitional fossils have ever been found. Each time one is brought forward, it later turns out to be a hoax. One of the more famous hoaxes was the Piltdown Man. The Neanderthal Man turned out to be a *Homo sapiens* with rickets and arthritis. Students can pursue www.answersingenesis.org for more information. To do a visual demonstration of this, put a cheap watch in a brown sack. Smash it with a hammer. Spill out the contents. Which is more logical—that these pieces will gradually turn into a watch or that there is a master watchmaker?

Environmental Change and Extinction

Adaptation is a very important skill for teachers to learn. We must learn to change a lesson to adapt to the needs of a class. God expects Christians to make adaptations regularly in order to bring the Gospel to those who do not yet know and believe. 1 Corinthians 9:22–23 describes the kind of adaptations Paul made for the sake of bringing the Gospel to more and more people. (8.2.5.5)

• Carefully explain to students the difference between macroevolution, the idea that living things evolve into new species, and microevolution, the idea that within a species an organism may adapt. Have students create a chart showing the difference between the two types of evolution. Then, have students find Bible verses beyond Genesis 1–2 that point to God's creation of the universe and all life.

• Create cards that have the names of animals from different climates on them. On another set of cards, write the names of different climate zones. Have students draw an animal card and a climate zone card. Have students explain why an animal would not be able to survive in a different climate. Use this as a springboard to discuss how God has placed us in places where we can thrive.

Extinction, Factors Causing

In Genesis 1:28, God put people in charge of His creation. We know what the result was (Romans 8:17–25). As a result of our sin, the entire world is oppressed. As you teach this standard to your students, remind them that although we have not taken good care of God's creation, we can give thanks to God that we have forgiveness through Jesus Christ. (8.2.5.6)

• Research an extinct species, specifically looking for causes of why the species went extinct. Share your findings with the class. As you and your classmates present, take note of the number of extinctions due to human causes.

• Design a poster making Law and Gospel applications to the topic of extinction. Because of sin—which brought death and, therefore, extinction into the world—we were condemned. But because of Jesus, we have life again. Although we can't bring back those organisms that are extinct, we can preserve the rest of God's creation as He has preserved us.

NATURAL SCIENCES

8.3   Eighth-grade students in Lutheran schools will understand concepts related to the natural sciences.

8.3.1   Space Studies

Universe and Its Galaxies

Scripture tells us that God created all of the stars (Genesis 1:16). It also goes on to tell us that these stars had their place alongside the other bodies of the universe, such as the sun and the moon. As you teach this lesson, ask students to look at how the stars are portrayed in the Bible, and help them to understand and appreciate the power and beauty of God's grace. (8.3.1.1)

• Using a resource, construct a model of the Milky Way and explain the estimated size of our galaxy. Research how many known galaxies are in the universe. Tell how these figures were determined. Read Genesis 22:1–19, and reflect on and explain this object lesson used by God and its message to Abraham.
• Research different types of galaxies by shape. Describe each galaxy shape with a model of a known galaxy with that shape. If possible, in the key for the model, tell how many actual stars each star in the model represents. Underneath each model, list the galaxy's name and the estimated number of stars in the galaxy. Then, read Genesis 22:17 and Deuteronomy 4:15–20, and compare how God used the stars in the Bible to make His will known to His people.

Light-Years and Interstellar Distances

Light-years are tremendous distances to cover. There is no way that a human can travel from Earth to the nearest star because of the great distance. With present technology, it would take generations to reach even the nearest star. The same is true of salvation. No person on his or her own can achieve salvation (John 14:6; Acts 4:12; Romans 8:5–11). Therefore, God breached the distance between sin and God and drew us close to Him once again. Stress that God has closed this vast distance for us by sending us His Son. (8.3.1.2)

• Research the nearest five stars to Earth. Identify how far each of the stars is in light-years and then figure out how far one light-year is in linear miles. Assuming that a space traveler has an average life span of eighty years and that the ship of the space travelers travels at 22,000 miles an hour, determine how many years it would take to reach the nearest star. How many generations would it take to reach the nearest star and return to Earth with information about the star? Read Luke 16:19–31, and reflect on the great distance that separates heaven and hell and the danger of being separated from God's grace. Write a prayer thanking God for sending Jesus to close the distance separating fallen humanity from God.
• Identify the distance that a light-year measures. Research the Milky Way and Earth's position in the Milky Way. Determine how many light-years it would take to reach the nearest edge of the Milky Way. Then, research what galaxy is beyond that point and the number of light-years it would take to reach the next galaxy. Read Matthew 28:16–20, and reflect on God's great power to be with us not only as we travel great distances but throughout time itself. Write a paragraph reflecting on God's love for you as expressed in Psalm 8.

Solar System, Planets, Satellites, Comets, and Asteroids

Scripture tells us that God created the heavenly bodies (Genesis 1:1, 1:16; Deuteronomy 4:15–20). Further, He gave these heavenly bodies a purpose. The sun gives us energy daily to support our physical needs. While God didn't tell us the purpose of these other bodies in the heavens, He did tell us that they were good (Genesis 1:18). God once spoke of His power over the heavenly bodies in these words to Job: "Can you bind the chains of the Pleiades or loose the cords of Orion? Can you lead forth the Mazzaroth in their season, or can you guide the Bear with its children? Do you know the ordinances of the heavens?" (Job 38:31–33). Stress that much of creation will remain a mystery until God chooses to reveal it to us. (8.3.1.3)

• On index cards, make study guides for learning the heavenly bodies of our solar system and those heavenly bodies that pass through it. Include on each card the name of the heavenly body, such as Mars or asteroid, and information about the heavenly body. Be sure to include all of the planets, size of planets, distances from the sun, length of orbits, how many moons (if any), and composition of the heavenly bodies. Read Genesis 1, and identify the heavenly bodies about which God spoke. What did He say about these heavenly bodies? In your opinion, what purpose do they serve?
• Make a PowerPoint presentation about the solar system and heavenly bodies that pass through our solar system. On each slide present a picture, the size of the body, its location in the solar system, and its composition. If the body is a planet, also add orbit information, such as time and distances. Read Luke 24:50, and reflect on the spiritual nature of God. Where is heaven?

Solar System, Motions within Relating to Days, Years, Seasons, Eclipses, Tides, and Moon Cycles

Scripture tells us that God created the Earth and all of its creatures in six days (Genesis 1). Therefore, God gave importance to a single day. As our Earth rotates on its axis and circles the sun, we are able to record days and years. The life of a Christian can also be measured in time and eternity (Ecclesiastes 3:2). Psalm 121:8 records the blessing, "The LORD will keep your going out and your coming in from this time forth and forevermore." Remind students that God chose us before the beginning of time to be His own and to live with Him in eternity (Ephesians 1:1–10). (8.3.1.4)

• Make a graph comparing the length of the seasons in relationship to Earth's orbit around the sun. Also include the fact that the Earth is tilted on its axis, and show how this affects the Northern and Southern Hemispheres. Make a graph for each of the planets showing distance from the sun, rotation periods, and temperature extremes. Read Ecclesiastes 3:1–8, and reflect on the times that occur in life. How does living a life that revolves around God change the way Christ's followers act and react during each of these times?
• Make a chart showing the different phases of the moon. Using a light source, a small ball, and a light colored background, demonstrate how light reflected from the moon changes as the moon revolves around the Earth. Read Matthew 24:29–30, and think about Christ's second coming and the mighty power of God. What force would it take not only to destroy the sun but also to make the billions of stars fall from the sky? Read 1 Thessalonians 5:1–11. Why can we find comfort in and even look forward to this great event? How are we to live as we look forward to this day?

Gravity and Planetary Motion

When God created the sun, He made it the center of our solar system. Because there is a direct relationship between the mass an object has and its gravitational force, the sun stabilizes the entire solar system, keeping the planets from sailing off into space. In the same manner, God keeps us from drifting into the emptiness of sin (Romans 6:22–23; Revelation 1:4–6). Stress how God—the Father, Son, and Holy Spirit—keeps us close to Him. (8.3.1.5)

• By God's design, the mass of planets in our solar system and their distances from the sun are factors in keeping the planets in orbit around the sun. What is the ratio of the mass of the sun to the mass of each of the planets? How does the combined mass of all of the planets in Earth's solar system compare to the mass of the sun? What do these comparative masses tell you about the sun's gravitational attraction?
• Research the mass of the sun and the masses of Mars and Earth. Then find the ratios between the mass of the sun and the individual masses of the Earth and Mars. Suppose that Earth and Mars exchanged orbits. How would Earth's gravity change? Predict what the Earth's gravity would be if it were in Mars's orbit. Write a prayer praising God for His creation and preservation of the universe.

Star, Life Cycle of a

The life cycle of a star shows the great power and patience of our Lord. Stars decay over such a long time period that humans with such a limited life span see little change as our sun goes through its life cycle. Point out that the life cycle of a Christian will outlast all of the stars in the universe (Matthew 24:29–30; 25:46; John 3:35–36). (8.3.1.6)

• Name the different-size stars in the universe. Compare and contrast the different life cycles of the stars. How long is the lifespan of each of the stars? What happens to each star at its death? Read John 3:35–36, and compare the life span of a star to the life span of a Christian.
• Describe the projected life span of our sun. What will happen to our sun as it reaches an end of its life span? What will happen to the Earth at that time? Read 2 Peter 3, and reflect on the end of the Earth. Write a paragraph telling what it means to you that God's almighty power surpasses even that of all of the stars in the universe.

Planets, Revolution of

Scripture tells us that our proximity to God is important (Hebrews 10:22). Because a planet's distance from the sun determines the planet's temperature, its position is important. The fact that a planet turns on an axis determines how much energy certain parts of a planet receive at a given time. Point out that God draws us near to Himself through the means of grace—the Word and the Sacraments. (8.3.1.7)

• Make a model of the solar system that shows the orbit of the first four planets of our solar system. Be sure to accurately scale the model to show distances at any specific point of the orbits. Also, list the length of the solar years of the planets. What do you notice about the solar years of the planets in relation to their distances from the sun? Read Luke 13:6–9, and explain the parable of the fig tree and what it means for us that our Lord and Savior is willing to wait a year for results.
• Compare and contrast the solar years of each of the planets. Then, make a graph showing the relationship between a planet's distance from the sun and the length of the planet's solar year. Is there a

common ratio that would let astronomers hypothesize as to the existence and whereabouts of additional planets in our solar system? Read Hebrews 10:19–25. Write a short theme explaining the power and motivation by which God's people "draw near with a true heart in full assurance of faith" (Hebrews 10:22).

Moon, Phases of

We see the energy of the sun reflected off the moon's surface differently depending on the position of the Earth and moon in relation to the sun. We also see different aspects of Jesus as the light of the world. His followers reflect Him to others. Jesus let His light shine upon us through the words and actions of His first disciples, be they fishermen, tax collectors, or workers in other professions (John 1:35–50; Matthew 9:10–13; Luke 5:1–11). (8.3.1.8)

• Using different sizes of Styrofoam balls and a light source and a solid background, make a model that demonstrates the movement of the Earth and moon around each other and provides the phases of the moon that we observe from Earth. Indicate the length of each moon phase and its frequency. Read Matthew 9:10–13 and John 1:35–50. Discuss how we see Sonlight reflected through the actions of Jesus' disciples.
• Make a drawing of the moon's different phases. Beneath each moon phase, explain the position of the moon and Earth in relation to the sun. Give additional details concerning the length of each moon phase and how long it takes to complete a moon phase cycle. Read Mark 6:7–13, which tells how Jesus sent out disciples to share Jesus as the promised Messiah (John 14:6). List ways Jesus' disciples of today reflect the light of His love into the world around them.

Eclipses, Lunar and Solar

Eclipses in the Old Testament (Jeremiah, Ezekiel, Joel, Amos) always refer to judgment. Prophets refer to them as they call for repentance. This fearful sign represented coming cataclysms to pagans in ancient times as well. With today's rationalism, heavenly events like rainbows and eclipses no longer carry any religious meaning at all, perhaps with the exception of a still entrenched belief in the zodiac and stars. It is interesting then that Jesus talks about eclipses when He describes Judgment Day in Matthew 24:29. St. John also describes eclipses in his vision of the judgment in Revelation 6:12. As an exercise in the use of a concordance, have students look up passages that refer to the sun and moon being darkened and write up their conclusions. (8.3.1.9)

• Using an 18 X 24 paper, place two pins 4 inches apart in the center. Cut and tie a 12-inch string in a loop. Place a pencil vertically on the inside edge of the string, pulling away from the pins until taut. Move the pencil around both pins, keeping it taut. You end up with an ellipse, the path Earth takes around the sun. Use an unshaded electric lamp sun and a tennis ball moon in a dark room to demonstrate eclipses. Ask questions about this. Since the moon goes around the Earth each month, why don't we have an eclipse each month? (The moon orbit is tilted at a 5 degree angle and not always in a line with the sun and Earth.) Why are there more solar eclipses than lunar eclipses? Could God have set it up so there would be no eclipses? Why might God have created the sun, moon, and Earth positions so that there could be eclipses?
• Homework questions: If the sun is God and you are the Earth, what would the moon be in a solar eclipse? (What blocks you from God: sin.)

Tides, High and Low

After explaining the moon's gravitational pull that affects the tides, think about what good tides are. What good are they to intercoastal waterway shipping? to bridge engineers? to deep water channel workers? The Hebrew words for the reference to chaos in Genesis 1 is *tohu wa-bohu*. God changed *tohu wa-bohu* into a solar system so systematic that we can predict tides with accuracy. What is God doing with the *tohu wa-bohu* in our lives? (8.3.1.10)

• Thread a string through a spool. Tie a weight on each end of the string. Swing the topmost weight around in a circle. See if you can keep the weights balanced. The spinning top weight shows centrifugal force; the bottom one shows gravity. The high tide that occurs on the opposite side of the Earth from where the moon is pulling that tide by gravity is being affected by centrifugal force. What other balanced forces did God create? (internal and external air pressure in living things, prey and predator ecosystems, composer and decomposer systems, and convection currents)
• God has supplied us with natural resources for renewable energy, such as solar power, wind power, and water power, which includes tidal generators. How might the use of the renewable energy sources plus reduced consumption help us to be responsible Christian stewards? How would it affect our nation's dependence on foreign oil? In turn, what effect would this have on wars fought with the economy as a factor?

Tides, Spring and Neap, and the Position of Moon and Sun

Spring and neap tides are high and low tides magnified by the additional gravity of the sun. These tides can remind us of how we sometimes feel in the work of teaching God has sent us to do. God promised His Word would not return to Him empty (Isaiah 55:11); it would have the effects He intended. When you feel your labor is like plowing the sea, remember that when you are in line with God, His will is being done whether you see the high tide or not. (8.3.1.11)

• In your discussion of this objective, integrate the faith by placing a sign saying "strong" on one side of the room and "weak" on the other. Tape a line with masking tape on the floor between them. Ask classmates to stand on this continuum to answer these questions: What effect do TV ads have on what you'd like to buy? What effect do your friends have on what you choose to do? What effect do your parents have on how you judge right and wrong? What effect does your church have on your understanding of God? What effect does this school have on your thoughts about life? What effect does God have on your thoughts about death? What effect does God have on your thoughts about life?
• The power of moving water plays a significant role in the Bible. Title a bulletin board "Biblical Water Power," and challenge classmates to add sticky notes of any examples that they find (e.g., the flood, Jesus calling Himself the living water, Baptism, the Spirit hovering above the water at creation, the river of life in Revelation, the parting of the Red Sea, the parting of the Jordan River, the laver in the tabernacle).

85

Earth, Uneven Heating of

God provides us with all we need. A clear manifestation of this is in the rotation of the Earth and the tilt of its axis so that our planet would be unevenly heated and that we would have seasons. Point out that this concept is just another way that we can see God's providing hand in our daily lives. (8.3.1.12)

• If the sun were closer to the Earth, Earth's atmosphere would be methane. Comment on the statistical odds of our universe resulting from an accident.
• In history, there have been many cultures that worshiped the sun. Research these beliefs and report to the class. Read Revelation 21:23–24; John 1:3–5; 8:12; and 9:5. Journal about why the Son is far greater than the sun.
• Praise God with the words of Psalm 19.

Seasons, Progression of

We often like to think of life in terms of seasons. Teachers and students look at the quarter or semester system in their schools. Athletes have seasons, and even life itself has been described in terms of seasons, such as "the autumn of my years." Take comfort in knowing that Christ is there for all seasons. Stress God's unchangeable quality. Though everything around us may change, our God does not! (8.3.1.13)

• In Ecclesiastes 3:1–8, we read that God has given us a time and season for everything. Analyze your life in terms of seasons. What are you doing, or can you do, right now to serve the Lord? What can you do in the future?
• On a piece of paper, write the four seasons in four separate columns. In each column, on a scale of one to four, record the amount of heat and light you receive during each season. Record your activities during each season. After completing this, consider special new activities you could do during the different seasons as service to God.

Daylight

There are many reasons why light doesn't reach the Earth. Axis tilt, cloud cover, inclement weather, and eclipse are all reasons why we may not get to see the sun. Make sure that in your teaching, you always show the Son. Stress that just as the sun is the source of all life and energy on our planet, Jesus is the source of new and eternal life for all who believe. Explain to your students that as believers their actions, attitude, and words all witness Jesus Christ and His love to others. (8.3.1.14)

• In John 8:12, Jesus said that He is the light of the world. Journal about how brightly that light is shown in your life.
• After studying reasons why the Earth has different amounts of daylight, research through LCMS World Mission (accessible through www.lcms.org) to find out where the light of the world is most in need of being shared. As a class, write to missionaries in these areas, encouraging them as they let the light of Christ shine.
• Dramatize the demonstration of God's power and control over the sun in answer to Joshua's prayer, which is recorded in Joshua 10:12–14.

Daylight, Latitude, and Direction of the Earth's Axis

Some days it seems like we never receive light. The problems of the classroom or with parents can leave us feeling mired in darkness. Pray that your students will always see the light of Christ in your classroom, receive it in their hearts, and show this light to others. (8.3.1.15)

• Chart daylight hours for the period of a month. Depending on the time of the school year, note a gradual increase or decrease of daylight. The information can usually be found in your newspaper or online at www.weather.com. Segue into a discussion of planning for the day. Use Matthew

6:25–34 to begin a discussion on trust in the Lord and the need to leave our worries and concerns in the hands of our loving Savior.

• Study the behavior of light waves. Light waves can bend, but the tilt of the Earth on its axis will always guarantee that there will be areas that won't receive light. Spread the light of the world by writing and then distributing Gospel tracts.

8.3.2   Land and Water

Earth's Composition, Structure, and Processes

Scripture tells us of many instances when God made His presence known through nonliving parts of His creation. He shook the Earth at Jesus' death (Matthew 27:51). Through the flood, God expressed His anger during the days of Noah (Genesis 6–8), and He parted the sea (Exodus 14:21). Stress the many ways we see God's hand at work in our environment. (8.3.2.1)

• Take a collection of rock samples provided by your teacher, and sort the rocks into groups that you believe are similar. Use a scratch plate, a weak acid solution, and a hardness kit to test the characteristics of the rocks. Using a rock and mineral key, classify the rocks according to their characteristics. Read Genesis 6–8, and hypothesize how the kind of weathering associated with the great flood would affect soft rock. Explain how such erosion could change the face of the Earth.

• Take a 12-inch square piece of corrugated cardboard and place it on top of several round dowel rods. Then, take a deck of playing cards and build a small house-like structure on top of the cardboard. After the card structure is finished, slowly push against the cardboard, moving the entire structure. Record what happens. Next, if the cards have not already tumbled, run the cardboard structure up against a thicker piece of cardboard so that the piece with the structure rises up on top of the other cardboard. Record the results. Continue in this manner until the card structure collapses. Think about how the Earth's tectonic plates place fixed structures at risk. Think of the house of cards as your life and the structure on which it is built as rock. If the rock is not firm, what would happen? Read Matthew 7:24–27. Sing the beloved hymn "Rock of Ages."

Earth Systems and the Atmosphere

Scripture tells us that God will provide for us (Matthew 6:25–34) and not to worry. Throughout the Bible, God provided for His people (Exodus 16:34–35). He promises never to leave or desert us (Matthew 28:20). God continually provides for our physical needs through natural cycles and our spiritual needs through the fulfillment of His plan for our salvation. (8.3.2.2)

• Design a chart showing the water cycle for North America. Explain where the moisture comes from and how our freshwater streams are dependent on the oceans. Next, hypothesize how North America's climate would change if the water cycle ended. What states would feel the effects first? Which states would still have an adequate water supply? All negative climatic conditions occur as a consequence of the fall of humanity into sin. Read Deuteronomy 28:15–24, and reflect on the warning against disobeying God.

• Place 100 milliliters of water into four different containers. Place one of the containers on the windowsill, place a second container near a light source, and place the other two containers around the room. Design a data table to collect evidence on the evaporation rate of the water. Write a 300–600-word report on what you believe would happen to your local community if water was not replaced by natural means and if the temperature of your community increased each year. Read Matthew 24:3–21. Of what coming occurrence do famines, earthquakes, and other troubling climatic conditions remind us?

Tectonic Plates (Crust, Magma)

Many places in Scripture warn us about the dangers of our inner self (Psalm 51:5–6; Romans 7:18). In examining the power of tectonic plates and the tremendous forces of the outer Earth's core, we can easily draw a comparison with the terrible power of sin (the slowly moving but destructive magma of the outer core) and the pressure it puts upon our lives (the tectonic plates). Stress that God is the only force capable of counteracting sin's destructive force and preventing destructive eruptions and quakes (Romans 8:1–4). (8.3.2.3)

• Using the Internet or another resource, research recent earthquakes and the destruction those earthquakes have caused, including secondary effects such as tsunamis and landslides. Write a 300–500-word report on the tectonic plates involved, explaining why earthquakes happen. Read Romans 8:1–17, and then write a one-page theme on the destructive power of sin, which was overcome for us by Christ Jesus.

• Open a box of Saltine crackers, and remove several crackers. Push a piece of corrugated cardboard against the crackers. Record your results, and write a hypothesis about why the crackers broke. Then, make an analogy between the crackers and cardboard as being tectonic plates and how the results are similar to the factors that cause earthquakes. Consider how the stronger plate (the cardboard) overpowered the smaller plate. Think about how Jesus conquered Satan with His death and resurrection. Read Matthew 28:1–10. Choose and sing an Easter hymn that focuses on the conquering power of Christ over sin, death, and Satan's power.

Tectonic Plates and Geological Events (Earthquakes, Volcanoes, Hot Spots, Mountain Building)

As tectonic plates cause productive processes that build up land masses, such as volcanic eruptions and mountain building, Scripture tells us that the Holy Spirit is the force that moves people and grows and builds God's Church (Acts 4:23–31). As

• Using the Internet or another resource, research the Ring of Fire and identify the tectonic plate action that provides the energy for volcanic action. Write a 300–500-word report on recent volcanic eruptions along the area. Identify the different types

we are filled with the Holy Spirit, we come to realize the truth, and as disciples, we spread God's Word. Stress the power of the Holy Spirit. (8.3.2.4)

of volcanoes along the Ring of Fire and the types of eruptions that might be suspected. Read Acts 4:23–31, and compare the forces of tectonic plates and the moving and working of the Holy Spirit.
• Research volcanoes, and on an outline of a world map, plot the volcanoes that are considered active. Compare the location of the active volcanoes with the location of tectonic plates. What conclusion can be drawn about the relationship of active volcanoes with the force of tectonic plate movement? Compare how faith is spread through the working of the Holy Spirit to the volcanic action and formations created by tectonic plate movement. Read Acts 9:17–31 and 17:6.

Earth, Surface and Interior

Scripture is filled with incidences where Jesus used parables to help people understand a deeper meaning (Matthew 13). These parables helped Jesus' disciples and those others He taught better understand those things that they could not see: faith, heaven, and salvation. In science, models are used to explain things too great to be seen, like the Earth, and too small to be seen, like the atom. As you teach this lesson, point out that we have learned more about the Earth and the physical world as our eyes have been opened by knowledge and technology. Tell students that as we study the Bible, we grow in knowledge that gives us a clearer understanding of God and His will and purpose for us. (8.3.2.5)

• Make a model of the Earth using a balloon, papier-mâché, and colored markers. After the papier-mâché dries, measure the model and draw the continents to scale. Color in the continents and oceans. Add the major islands. When you are finished, read Matthew 13:1–23. Think about how God helped us see parables through eyes of faith.
• Cut an apple evenly in half. Use the cut apple to explain the different parts of inner Earth. Use food coloring to mark the different parts of Earth's interior: the crust, the mantle, the outer core, and the inner core. Cover the model with a clear clinging plastic wrap. Prepare an oral presentation for the class. Before the presentation, read Genesis 1 and reflect on God's great wisdom and power as He created the Earth and filled it with marvelous creatures. Notice how God was pleased with His creation and instill that joy into your presentation.

Tectonic Plate Motions, Forces Driving

Heat plays an important role in the formation of many rocks. The Holy Spirit plays an essential role in faith development (Matthew 3:11–12) and builds up Christians in a way that can remind us of how thermal energy forms metamorphic rock. Scripture tells us that Christians change and become stronger as they are firmly bonded by faith (Matthew 15:28; 21:21; Mark 10:52). Help students understand that as God used His power to create processes that continually change the Earth, He also uses faith to change and strengthen us. (8.3.2.6)

• Research the life cycle and characteristics of metamorphic rock, and compare metamorphic rocks to sedimentary rocks. Especially focus on which rocks are most affected by weathering and other forces of nature. Prepare an oral presentation explaining how the heating process hardens metamorphic rock. Think about how God has used the difficult times in your life to strengthen you, much as thermal energy has strengthened metamorphic rock during its life cycle. Create a devotion on this theme based on Isaiah 41:10.
• Using poster board and markers or colored pencils, construct a two-dimensional model of a shield

volcano, including a written section explaining how rock becomes magma, magma becomes lava, and lava becomes rock. Write a paragraph making a comparison between the formation of metamorphic rock and this cycle in the life of a Christian: sin to conviction, conviction to recognition of a need for salvation, and then faith and our new existence as "living stones" (1 Peter 2:4–5).

Landform Creation (Weathering, Erosion, Crustal Deformation, Volcanic Activity, Deposition)

Scripture records many times when God used natural forces in conjunction with His efforts to change and guide people. With Jonah, God used a great storm (Jonah 1:1–17). Jesus once walked on water and calmed the wind (Mark 6:47–51). Saul's conversion began with a bright light (Acts 22:6). Sometimes even those natural forces that seem destructive can also have great benefits. As erosion washes away topsoil in one place, it deposits it in another, forming new land. In the same manner, God sometimes uses destructive forces to further His plan (Matthew 28:2). Point out that for every destructive force there is also a positive benefit, just as through death comes eternal life. (8.3.2.7)

• Take a large rectangular plastic basin, and drill several holes into the bottom for water to drain. Fill the basin with about 2 inches of sand, putting a filter over the holes to keep the sand from draining. Tilt the basin by supporting one end with books. Pour water from a 2-liter water bottle near the high end, and watch how the water erodes the sand. Remember to place an empty container under the open holes to catch the water. Record your results and predict what would happen if this model was used on a large scale. Use this model as a visual aid in a devotion based on Matthew 7:24–27.
• Using the same basin from activity one, fill it with 2 inches of sand. Gently tilt the container, add grass seed, and then add a small amount of water. Watch for a couple of days. Take a cup of topsoil, and put it into a 2-liter water container filled with water. Repeat the process for several times until topsoil covers the sand. Observe to see if the grass seed takes hold. Record your results. While you wait, read Mark 4:1–20, and think about how God sows the seeds of faith into good soil. Talk about the characteristics of good soil. Identify the characteristics of good spiritual soil.

Rock-Layer Formation (Folding, Faulting, and Uplifting)

Just as the location of rocks from rock layers may not be a good indicator of the age of a rock formation, Scripture tells us that position or age is not necessarily a good measure of faith or importance in God's kingdom (Isaiah 11:6; Mark 9:36; 9:42). As you teach this lesson on rock formations, stress that to God everyone is important (2 Corinthians 5:15). (8.3.2.8)

• Using the Internet or another resource, research rock layers. Compare and contrast folding, faulting, and uplifting in terms of location and age. Explain why a rock layer may not be a good indicator of the age of a rock layer. Think about the faith development within your family. Is age a good indicator of faith? Read Mark 9:36–37. Read, discuss, and apply 1 Timothy 4:12.
• On a piece of poster board, draw a model of rock formations that show folding, faulting, and uplifting. Label the different parts, and write a

brief paragraph for each process, explaining the age of each layer from youngest to oldest. Think about the process of rock formation, and compare that to the change in formation through which a Christian goes. Is the oldest Christian always the greatest? Read Luke 22:24–30.

Plate Boundaries (Transform, Divergent, and Convergent)

Our students are daily being pushed and pulled in multiple directions. Sometimes those forces build into tremendous explosions of emotional outbursts. Sometimes they are pulled apart and left with a deep trench of despair. Encourage students to turn to God during those times when Satan is working especially hard to come between them and Jesus. Our great and powerful God has promised to help us in our weakness (Romans 8:26–27). (8.3.2.9)

• Take a roll of clay and flatten it out with a rolling pin until the clay is approximately ⅛-inch thick. Next, grab two ends of the clay and pull evenly in opposite directions. Continue pulling until the clay separates. Record what the clay looks like. Is the break a straight line or jagged? Where did the tear first begin? Next, roll the clay back into a ball and repeat the process. Only this time, roll the clay into a thicker sheet. Were the results the same? Use the results to compare against the type of plate boundaries that form ocean trenches. Think about the division Satan tries to place between us and God. Create a work of art to visually underscore God's promise recorded in Romans 8:38.

• Take a roll of clay, and flatten it with a rolling pin. Take the sheet of clay and place it on a piece of wax paper. Cut a piece of corrugated cardboard to approximately the same size as the sheet of clay. Working with a partner, slowly push the two plates together until the clay rolls on top of the cardboard and folds form. Relate this type of plate boundary with the formation of mountains. Think about the opposing forces in your life, and reflect on how God has helped you through times of stress and opposition. Read 1 Peter 1:3–9.

Convection Currents within the Mantle and Movement in Earth's Crust

Genesis 1:9–10, which discusses God gathering the waters in one place, gave rise to Antonio Snider's theory of horizontal continent movement back in 1859. Most scientists of that time believed the Earth was shrinking. Since then the theory of plate movement due to convection currents has become widely accepted. Currently, some scientists like Dr. John Baumgardner advocate catastrophic plate tectonics caused by rapid subduction during the flood rather than the gradual movement theory that assumes billions of years. You can find more information on this by researching catastrophic plate tectonics. The point is that science is still not in complete agreement on this subject. Students need to be aware of the bias of textbook

• Sometimes as students study Earth's core, questions like "Where is hell?" and "Is there really a physical hell?" come up. The idea of hell in the center of our physical Earth probably came from the Greek word for hell *tartarus*, which means "infernal region" (2 Peter 2:4). The Hebrew word in Deuteronomy 32:22 translated "hell" is *sheol*, which means unseen state. Check a concordance to find a significant number of references to this place, including statements made by Jesus who went there soon after His resurrection.

• Compare and contrast the water cycle and the convection cycle. The cycle of rising up and sinking down is also true of relationships. All relationships have their up and down cycles, including the one

writers who don't even mention other theories! Christians also have a bias—the assumption that God had and has a hand in Earth's operations! (8.3.2.10)

with God. But these ups and down occur only from our human side. God does not cycle in relationships. He is faithful with grace and mercy, even when we do not perceive His presence. Explore this aspect of cycling by asking questions. In the relational cycle with your parents, are you up or down at the moment? How about them with you—up or down? In the relational cycle with God, are you up or down at the moment? How about God with you?

Igneous, Sedimentary, and Metamorphic Rocks, Formation of

Your science textbook may state that the rocks of Earth come from the interchange of lava and magma over a billion years. Non-Christians either assume a god who created the original big bang and then left or simply dismiss the initiation phase and move on past it. To believe in a God who began the universe with words, creating mature galaxies, mature rocks, mature plants, animals, and people who were already beyond birth is never considered. Genesis 1–2 are written off as simple myths for the less intelligent. Have you ever wondered why God doesn't give us His recipe for creation? If He did, would any human be able to read it? (8.3.2.11)

• Your teacher will pass out a sack of rocks to small groups. Sort these rocks into the three categories. Deduce the physical properties of each category. From this, groups should diagram similarities and differences between the three groups. (One similarity is that they are all created by God.)
• If you were one of the three kinds of rocks, which would you be and why? Write your thoughts on paper or in your lab notebooks. Volunteers may share. Jesus called Peter's faith the rock of His Church. Which type of rock do you think that could be and why?

Rock Cycle

Rocks move without their own volition. Wind and water erode them to bits and move them as they will. Some fall into places where heat and pressure force them into denser rocks, which can slowly be moved toward the intense heat of Earth's magma. There they melt and move through the convection currents operating on them perhaps to eventually be pushed up into the air. They cool and become solid rocks again. People sometimes think they are being moved by forces beyond their control. Circumstances of life certainly influence physical life, but no one else controls one's soul. We are not in bondage since Jesus kept His soul pure in spite of forces tempting Him to sin. (8.3.2.12)

• Create a story for a single piece of granite, beginning with its creation by God. Move it through erosion and so on all through the rock cycle. You might suggest that the rock's life cycle ends with that day God destroys the Earth (2 Peter 3:10) to create a new heaven and Earth.
• Track cause and effect in the rock cycle. Label each with "God-controlled" or "Human-controlled." Some would protest that this is actually natural law, rather than specifically God-overseen. Science texts credit natural law as a force in order to separate Church and State in public education. As a Christian, you don't have to look at the issue that way!

Minerals, Characteristics of

Geologists determine the minerals in rock by slicing off a sliver to look at microscopic crystals, checking with a magnet for iron or nickel, and dropping acid on it to test for carbonates. The pur-

• Make memory cairns. Take fifteen to twenty stones. In permanent marker, write a few words on each stone that note past events of special spiritual significance. Full anecdotes for each can be

pose of this is mineral identification to provide knowledge of rock components and guess where this rock has been. God allows Satan to test us too (Job 1). God is all-knowing. Why would He need proof to determine our character or faith? When Jesus was led in the desert to be tested, He already knew His nature as God-man (Matthew 4). Maybe you've wondered about the point of that forty-day experience. (Not all pain comes from testing; some is the consequence of sinful actions.) There are at least two choices: (1) God is not in total control so sometimes evil triumphs, or (2) permitting pain serves some ultimate purpose. God's Word teaches the latter. Consider the importance of us knowing Jesus triumphed over every possible test Satan threw His way. Consider also that being obedient to God even unto death was part of Jesus' glorification! (Being obedient to pleasant actions doesn't really signify the way obedience to tough times does.) Perhaps testing is the only way to build faith muscles. Testing can build up the soul, unlike the testing of rocks that diminishes them. (8.3.2.13)

written in a prayer journal. Cement each cairn together. You might display these at church with an explanation in the bulletin. Like the minerals that are in the rock, memories of events in which we recognized God at work are in our souls.
• Challenge students to create a rock rap. Here's a start:
He will, He will
Rock you . . . rock you.
Zoom in close and you will find
Lava rock got left behind
On Earth's crust ba-salt He spread.
"Let there be," is what He said,
Took some granite in His hand,
Mountains rose at His command.
He will, He will
Rock you . . . Rock you.

Water, Distribution and Circulation of

God has designed a sustainable water purification system. All the chemical gunk in water is eventually purified either by plants (a tree can put off 260 liters of pure water a day) or by distillation through evaporation and condensation. If you had to manage a global system of mega million kiloliters of water, could you even dream up how leaves could do part of the work? Leaf power! (8.3.2.14)

• Do the following demonstration: weigh together seven plastic sandwich bags, seven pebbles, and seven twist ties. Record the weight in grams to the nearest tenth of a gram. Now place each plastic bag around a similar-size leaf on a tree nearby. Place a pebble in each bag, and then use the twist tie to secure the bag to the leaf's branchlet. Make a good seal. At the same time the next day, carefully remove each bag, replacing the twist tie back to seal each bag. Weigh all bags together again. Hypothesize to explain the weight difference. Design an experiment to test your theory. Trees are an incredible invention of God—for soil erosion prevention, for the CO_2–O_2 cycle, for animal and plant habitats, and for sheer beauty. Transpiration is now added to the list.
• If you Google "hydrologic cycle," you will find some fantastic visuals of the water cycle as well as distribution figures. Make an overhead of the following under the title "What God Did with the Water He Separated from Dry Ground." When you first show the chart, cover the percentages and let other students predict the order.

Water Source	Water Volume in cu. Km	Percent
Oceans/Seas	1,338,000,000	96.5
Groundwater	23,400,000	1.7
Lakes	176,400	.013
Soil Moisture	16,500	.001
Ground Ice/Permafrost	300,000	.022
Atmosphere	12,900	.001
Swamp	11,470	.00008
Ice Caps/Glaciers/Perm Snow	24,064,000	1.74
Rivers	2,120	.0002
Biological Water	1,120	.0001

Water, Fresh and Salt

In Matthew 5:13–16, Jesus refers to us as salt and also as the light of the world. Jesus explains that if salt is no longer salty, it is good for nothing. Consider your own salinity. Is your faith evident to those around you? (8.3.2.15)

• Have glasses of water with varying ratios of salinity from fresh water to supersaturated. Taste the samples, cleaning your palette each time, to see when you can first notice the salt water. Identify samples in which the salt water is almost immediately noticeable. Read and reflect on Matthew 5:13. Choose the sample containing the concentration of salt most closely relating to your current level of spiritual growth and maturity.
• Look at a container of fresh water and a container of salt water with a low level of salinity. Can you recognize a difference between the two? Explain that appearances can be deceiving and that we can't always tell a Christian by outward appearance. Write a paragraph answering the question "What makes someone a Christian?"

Earth's Resources, Wise Use of

Although God put us in charge of His creation, we have failed. As a result, we continue to strive for cleaner fuels and less reliance on fossil fuels. Stress the need for ethical, Christlike stewards of God's creation and the power of the Holy Spirit at work through the means of grace helping us to live for Jesus. (8.3.2.16)

• Identify ways you can help reduce the amount of trash at home and school.
• Research petroleum and coal formation through the Institute of Creation Research (www.icr.org) to find out how coal and petroleum evidence creation, a young Earth, and a great flood.

Resources, Local and Impact of Transportation

You may feel a pain when you buy gasoline. Maybe the prices are high enough that you are considering alternative transportation. The resources that we have here on Earth may diminish, but our spiritual resources will never run out. Remind your students that their spiritual resources in Christ Jesus are infinite (John 4:13–14). (8.3.2.17)

• Devise a list of ways to help conserve resources as wise stewards of God's creation (Genesis 1:28).
• Through interviews, research the price of gasoline in your area over the past five years. Make a connection between the law of supply and demand and gas prices. Point to highs in gas prices, and speculate as to what caused the spike. Use this as a springboard to discuss ethics. How should Christians in business deal with pricing issues?

Pollution (Smoke, Smog, Sewage), Effects of

Unfortunately, much of the pollution in our world is permanent. We cannot completely remove some of the toxins in our environment. Comment that sin pollutes our entire lives. Jesus removed the eternal consequences of the pollution of sin through His life, death, and resurrection (Psalm 103:12). (8.3.2.18)

• Research the causes of pollution in your area. After you and your classmates report to the class, theorize on ways to clean up the pollution in the area, since as stewards of God's creation, we are to take good care of our environment.
• There are many clean fuel resources that are being explored. Write a paper chronicling the advancement of clean fuels in our nation. As a part of the paper, analyze why developing and using clean fuels is an important part of good Christian stewardship.

8.3.3   Weather and Seasons

Atmospheric Layers

When God created the heavens and the Earth, He made the Earth's atmospheric layers so that they would protect the Earth from outside harmful effects. Earth is always in danger from collisions with asteroids or comets, solar flares, or other destructive forces, but the real danger is not from elements of our solar system. Satan is the element that puts us all at risk (1 Peter 5:8–9). Stress that God protects us from all harm and that He insulates us from Satan much as the Earth's atmosphere insulates us from outside forces. (8.3.3.1)

• Draw a model of the Earth's atmospheric layers. Draw the model to scale, and label each layer. Identify the function of each layer, and then write a report to present to the class, explaining the function of each of the Earth's layers. Especially identify atmospheric pressure at each level and protection of harmful effects outside the Earth's atmosphere, such as radiation and meteoroids. Read Ephesians 6:10–18, and compare how God protects us from Satan to how the Earth's atmosphere protects us from solar radiation.
• Using the Internet or another resource, collect data on the Earth's atmosphere and the atmosphere of Mars. How are they similar? How are they different? Compare winds, atmospheric pressure, atmospheric compositions, temperatures, and precipitation. Read Genesis 1:26–31 and Matthew 6:25–26, and reflect on how important the atmosphere is to the birds. Could a bird fly on Mars? Could it breathe in Mars's atmosphere? Why or why not? Write a prayer thanking and praising God for His love and care for us.

Latitude and Climate

Location is extremely important to the climate of a region. Because the sun is the source of all energy on Earth, it directs the global weather conditions our planet experiences. Because Earth tilts and rotates on an axis, we have four seasons. God created the world and it was good (Genesis 1), but the fall into sin has resulted in global consequences. Many places on Earth have especially harsh conditions. Good land for crops has been

• Using the Internet or another resource, break up the continents by latitudes lines around the globe. Compile a list of data about each latitude that includes seasons, annual high and low temperatures, precipitation amounts, and amount of daylight. Read Deuteronomy 8:7–9, and reflect on the importance of location to the Earth's natural resources. Create a travel brochure advertising the highlights of your community, including a prayer

sought after throughout history (Deuteronomy 8:7–9). Point out that God has granted us growing seasons and climate that provides us with all we need to survive and thrive. (8.3.3.2)

thanking God for the blessings of your locality.
• You have decided to become a landowner by homesteading in Alaska. Research the latitude and climate that you will encounter. Make a list of items you will need for survival if you reach your homestead site, which is 100 miles north of Anchorage, during the month of May. What types of crops will you plant? How will you survive that first winter? How cold will the winter be? How long will your growing season be? Read Genesis 1:14 and 8:22. Find or draw pictures or take photographs to show the same landscape at different seasons of the year. Think about how important the seasons are for providing our needs.

Temperature and Precipitation

Since the fall into sin, people have had to struggle against the elements to produce the food needed for survival (Genesis 3:17–19). Because water is so important to growing crops, rivers and streams and rainfall have long been important factors in the wealth of a region. Wars have been fought over rich, well-watered lands. Droughts have caused great famines (Genesis 41:41–57) and changed the course of history. Lead your students to understand and appreciate God's hand in our weather and seasons. (8.3.3.3)

• Research simple weather instruments, and make a rain gauge. Set the rain gauge out on school grounds and record daily rainfall amounts for a month. Compare the collected data against norms for your area. Was there more or less rainfall during the collection period? Predict what would happen if your area received little or no rainfall for a five-year period. Read Genesis 41:41–57 and 50:20. Talk about how God worked to put Joseph in a position through which he could help and save God's people during a drought.
• Research rainfall amounts in the areas surrounding the Rocky Mountains in the United States. What are the rainfall amounts of states just west of the Rocky Mountains? What are the rainfall amounts of states just east of the Rocky Mountains? Hypothesize whether or not the Rocky Mountains play a factor in the annual rainfall amounts of these states. Draw a graph predicting how much more or less rainfall would fall upon the affected states if the Rocky Mountains were not present. Read Matthew 5:45. Write a paragraph explaining how God blesses both believers and nonbelievers through beneficial environmental conditions like sunshine and rain.

Volcanoes, Greenhouse Gases, and El Niño, Global Effects of

God has used global effects to get people's attention and to affect His will. The great flood (Genesis 7), mighty winds (Exodus 14), and earthquakes (Matthew 28:2) are all examples of global effects God used to further His plan. These incidents demonstrate God's awesome power in cre-

• Research the damage caused by the greatest tornado, greatest hurricane, greatest flood, greatest earthquake, and greatest volcanic eruption of the past 300 years. Write a report on the damages done to property and human life. Read Genesis 7, and compare the damage you investigated to that

ation. Stress that all of the combined power of humanity is feeble in comparison to the natural forces that God created. (8.3.3.4)

of the great flood.

• Research the last eruption of Mount St. Helens. Identify the local and global effects caused by the eruptions. Specifically, how much force was generated from the blast? How many lives were lost? What was the area of devastation? How were communities near the site affected? How was the global community affected? Read Exodus 14, and reflect on how God uses global effects to further His plan. Then make a list of the positive effects of each natural disaster. For example, floods deposit topsoil, and volcanoes make new islands and fertile soil. Make a list of good things God has brought about through bad things in your life (Romans 8:28).

Weather Patterns, Pressure Systems, Frontal Systems

The sun is the driving force behind weather. If the Earth weren't rotating, there would be just one system—warm air rising at the equator and flowing to the poles as cold polar air comes below it to replace warm air. But we do have the spin, uneven heating in various seasons, and water and land breezes and mountain influences. Such variety! All living creatures depend on a Creator who controls the sun and the weather (Job 38:22–26). Picture God chuckling as He also watches the weather forecast. (8.3.3.5)

• In North America, high pressure winds sink down clockwise while low pressure winds move up counterclockwise. Explain why that is. After reading Job 38:22–26, write about each process with a set of instructions from God to the wind.
• Interview a Christian meteorologist in your area who can bring along the readouts he or she uses to write up forecasts. What part does faith play in his or her life and work? Prepare questions in advance so that the questions you have time for are significant ones.

Hurricane, Tornado, and Thunderstorm Formation

Most people at some point in their lives wonder why God allows such tremendous natural forces to devastate the innocent. Some are quick to point a finger in judgment, thinking perhaps of the ten plagues in Egypt before the exodus. Others call it natural occurrences in which God does not choose to interfere. Neither satisfies the description of a loving God to many. God's love doesn't always fit our human definition of love as pleasuring, comforting, encouraging, and giving. God's definition of love is best seen in the Father's sacrifice of His only Son who accepted brutal torture while surrounded by hordes of gloating religious leaders and demons. In addition, He suffered our punishment, taking on every sin for every person ever to be alive. Since God's love includes obedience even to suffering and death, what then is the redeeming purpose of suffering? That's the real question and

• Compare wind speeds of typical hurricanes (75 miles per hour), tornadoes (125–300 miles per hour), and thunderstorms (40–50 miles per hour). A lightning bolt lasts only 1/10 of a second but has thirty million volts, which could light up all of New York City! Lightning heats the air around it to 20,000 degrees Fahrenheit! These are enormous forces! What other tremendous forces exist (the splitting of an atom, nuclear fusion, angel-power as in 2 Kings 19:35)? But greater than all these is the power of God's love in Christ Jesus, "Neither death nor life, nor angels nor rulers, nor things present nor things to come, nor powers, nor height nor depth, nor anything else in all creation, will be able to separate us from the love of God in Christ Jesus our Lord" (Romans 8:38–39).
• Work in small groups to make flow charts on the developmental steps leading to hurricanes,

a good one to explore, since it opens the door to this very common reason people give for not believing in Jesus. If you do not have your own answers, invite your pastor in for discussion as well as some of the church elders. (8.3.3.6)

tornadoes, and thunderstorms. As the atmospheric conditions occur, at what points could development be halted or dissipated? Make a similar flow chart for a relational squall, again showing at what points development can be halted or dissipated. Write a realistic anecdote of a possible storm situation for an eighth grader and parent, sibling, acquaintance, or classmate where such a halting point occurred. What role can prayer play in halting storms of any kind?

Weather Instruments (Barometers, Thermometers, Anemometers, Psychrometers)

We love technology! Advancements in technology have made our lives much better and safer. The technology that your class will study in conjunction with this standard has helped us predict weather patterns. Unfortunately, even with the best equipment, we still face problems. Stress that even with the best equipment, our efforts cannot be perfect because of sin. Thanks be to God in Christ that He is the perfection for us all. (8.3.3.7)

• Study weather-measuring devices. Then consider your faith. Do you have the faith of a thermometer or the faith of a thermostat? Thermometer Christians simply react to culture around them and change with the times. Thermostat Christians are the agents of change, changing all those around them to be like them. List the kind of activities that closely connect with each group.
• After analyzing these instruments, analyze the instruments that we use in connection with our faith life. Identify a Christian book, video, or CD that has helped you mature in your faith.

SCIENTIFIC PROCESSES AND APPROACHES

INFORMATION BY TOPIC

DISCUSSION POINTS/ACTIVITIES

8.4 **Eighth-grade students in Lutheran schools will understand concepts related to scientific processes and approaches**

8.4.1 **Scientific Methods**

Investigations, Procedure for Conducting

Scientific methods of investigation help us collect and organize data with less bias and greater accuracy. The Bible teaches us to collect information about God's plan for the redemption of humanity. It organizes the data and displays it conclusively, leaving no need for further efforts at finding the way to salvation (John 14:6). Stress that the Bible is God's Word. Through God's Word, the Holy Spirit brings us faith and salvation through the merits of Jesus Christ. (8.4.1.1)

• Design an experiment to determine which kind of soil would grow the best crop of corn. Make sure that you include developing a hypothesis, identifying appropriate tools for testing your hypothesis, and designing a system for collecting and displaying the data. Read John 11:25–27, and reflect on the miracles that Jesus performed and that were observed by His disciples. Such data from the Bible helps us form a powerful conclusion regarding Jesus as our Lord and Savior. List Jesus' miracles and categorize each as healing, control over natural forces, or bringing the dead back to life.

• Using a ball and jacks, design an experiment to test the speed and reflexes of five students in your class. Before beginning the experiment, check the background of your test subjects: their hobbies, interests, and special skills. Formulate a hypothesis and test it. Display your data and draw a conclusion that the data supports. Read John 2:1–11; Matthew 14:22–32; and Luke 9:10–17. What conclusion does this data support with regard to Jesus Christ?

Investigations, Sample and Control

Scripture tells us that throughout Jesus' ministry the Jewish leaders wouldn't accept Him as the Son of God. They tried to trick Him whenever they could (Matthew 12:22–37; 16:1–4; Mark 7:1–23). Encourage students to go to the Bible when circumstances or people test their faith, because it is our source of strength, encouragement, and answers. (8.4.1.2)

• A sample that is too small is highly susceptible to errors because of extremes of the data. Create a small data set, and include one number that is far larger or smaller than the remainder of the data set. Find the mean, median, and mode of the data. Next, drop the number outside the data set. Find the mean, median, and mode of the data. Compare the two sets of data. Which is more accurate? Read Mark 7:1–23, and reflect on how you would deal with someone who challenges that Jesus Christ is the Son of God. What would you use as a control?

• Create two sets of data each with a range of sixty-four. Include ten pieces of data in one set and thirty pieces of data in the second set. Find the mean, median, and mode of each of the two data sets. Which is the more accurate? Is the smaller data set more affected by the range than the larger set? Is so, why? Read Matthew 12:22–37, and reflect on why many people do not receive Jesus as their Lord and Savior. Is it because their data set is too limited?

Reliable Resources, Print and Nonprint

Information about research conducted by others is extremely important in forming a hypothesis. For the Christian, the Bible is the most important source of information regarding God's plan for salvation. God has given us history, poetry, and the key to eternal life within the Bible (examples of each: Genesis, Psalms, John). Stress the importance of going to the right source when seeking answers to the most important of life's questions. (8.4.1.3)

• Using the Internet, research various Earth biomes. Research ten different sites, and compare the biomes from each site. Is the information the same? If not, which do you believe is the most accurate? Write three or four paragraphs explaining how you could identify an accurate resource to use in forming your hypothesis. Read John 3:16, and then use the rest of the Bible to support the passage. Find three or four other passages that restate that Jesus Christ is the means of salvation for us and for all people.

• Research the greenhouse effect using the Internet and three other sources. Which do you consider the most reliable? Why? Which of the sources that you chose is most prone to errors? What safeguard could you use to ensure accuracy of information from these sources? Read Matthew 8:23–27 and Mark 4:35–41. How do these two accounts scientifically increase the validity of Jesus Christ as the Son of God?

Variables

Scripture tells us that there is only one way to reach heaven (Acts 4:12). In the sinful world of today, the emphasis on feeling better focuses on making oneself look better or feel more confident; however, God has given us the only true means of reaching heaven: Jesus Christ. Point out that Jesus is the only variable in our battle to overcome sin and the devil. (8.4.1.4)

• Consider that a scientist wants to design a new cleaner for removing stains on clothing. He decides to try different types of commercial cleanser to see which removes more stains. Then, he decides to also add a chemical of his own to several of the cleaning solutions. Why do the scientist's actions make it more difficult to determine what cleanser would work best? Read Acts 4:12. What is the one variable that cleans mankind from the stain of sin?

• Imagine that you design an experiment that will grow the largest coconuts. In one field, change the fertilizer and amount of water. In a second field, change the amount of water and sunlight. In the third field, change the soil type and fertilizer. After you gather your coconuts, you discover that the second field had the best coconuts. Can you reliably say what needs to be done in order to grow larger coconuts? Why or why not? Read Romans 6:23; John 3:16; and 11:25–26. What is the constant variable in these three passages? What is the result?

Data, Gathering, Interpreting, and Explaining

Scripture tells us that the disciples had difficulty seeing the big picture that Jesus painted for them even though Jesus clearly stated the He was the fulfillment of God's plan for the redemption of all people (2 Corinthians 5:21). Yet even Peter had difficulty understanding Jesus (Matthew 14:22–31; 16:23–28; 17:1–5). Stress that we must continually read Scripture so that we are able to know and trust in God and to interpret His will for our lives. (8.4.1.5)

• Design a simple experiment, such as flipping a quarter fifty times to determine whether or not it will land on heads and tails an equal number of times. Place the data in a data table, graph the information, and write a summery of what happened. Present the information to the entire class. Read Matthew 16:23–28, and write several paragraphs explaining why Peter was wrong for making the suggestion that he did.

• Using a deck of cards, design a simple experiment to see if your classmates have the ability to determine which card you have pulled from the deck. Make sure to test at least ten students and pull at least ten cards from the deck. Organize the data into a table, and graph the information. What does the information tell you? Read John 14:6; 11:25–26; and 6:40. Organize the information into a written summary to show what could be interpreted from these passages.

• Read Luke 12:54–59. Explain Jesus' comments about the inability of the teachers of the day regarding interpretation of signs (data).

Investigations Referencing Topographic and Geologic Maps

Scripture tells us that Jesus was from the "town of Nazareth in Galilee" but was born in Bethlehem (Luke 2:1–7). To better understand Scripture, it is important to get a sense of where Jesus was born and the extent of His ministry and the ministry of His disciples after His death and resurrection. As you teach using topographic and geologic maps, stress the extent of Jesus' ministry and how Christianity spread throughout the world beginning in such a small area. (8.4.1.6)

• Using maps from the Internet or another resource, research the deforestation of the Brazilian rainforest. How much area has been destroyed? What has replaced the area? How long is it estimated before the entire rainforest is destroyed? Why is the forest being destroyed? Will it be possible to replace the rainforest that has already been lost? Read Genesis 1:26, and reflect on how God would have us manage His creation. Write up a plan that you would initiate to ensure the survival of the rainforest.

• Using a topographic map of your neighborhood, pick several routes from one end of your neighborhood to the other. Which way will be the fastest? What natural and manmade obstacles will have to be overcome to cross your neighborhood? Read Exodus 14:17–31, and reflect on the obstacles the Israelites faced during their exodus from Egypt. How did God help them deal with the obstacles in their path?

Matter, History of Understanding, Work of Lavoisier, Antoine, and Curie, Marie and Pierre

Scripture helps us understand the basics of our human condition and God's plan for redemption, fulfilled in history through the person and work of Christ Jesus (Galatians 4:4). It is also the means of grace. Through God's Word, the Holy Spirit convicts us of our sin, leads us to repent, and works in us a saving faith in Jesus. (8.4.1.7)

• Research Antoine Lavoisier's contribution to the understanding of matter, and write a 300-word report to present to the class. What contributions did Lavoisier make? Why were they significant? Where were they made? How did they change the course of history? Read Matthew 1:1–16, and list some contributions that these historic figures made in furthering God's plan for the salvation of mankind.

• Marie and Pierre Curie did some of the pioneering work in the field of radioactivity, which fascinated them. Yet they did not recognize the devastating effects radioactivity was having on their health. Eventually Marie died from the results of exposure to radioactivity. Compare the consequences of the Curies' exposure to radioactivity with the consequences of all people's exposure to sin. Incorporate James 1:15 into your discussion.

Solutions to Scientific Problems, Constraints to

God's plan for our salvation put severe constraints on His Son who entered this world to walk among us as human. Jesus could call upon legions of angels (Matthew 26:52–54) at any time, but He chose to die upon a cross for the fulfillment of Scriptures in order to redeem and save us. During this time period, Jesus paid the cost for our sins and removed for all eternity its stain upon the soul of humanity. As you teach, stress how Jesus overcame the fall into sin by supplying Himself as a substitute sacrifice in our place. Jesus is the only solution for the supreme human problem of sin. (8.4.1.8)

• Write up a solution for the rising cost of using oil and gasoline by creating an alternate source of power. Research different alternative fuels, and make a list of the constraints that keep these sources from being used today, such as not enough power or too costly. Write up your own plan to counter these constraints, and provide an alternate source of power not dependent on fossil fuels. Read about Jesus' crucifixion in Matthew 26 and 27. Write how in one sense Jesus became an alternate sacrifice and restored fallen humanity into God's grace.

• You have decided to join the contest to build the first civilian space flight vehicle. Your vehicle must safely take two people into space and return them safely, and then the flight must be repeated again in a three-week period. Research vehicles that are currently being tested, and identify the obstacles the design must overcome in order to be effective. What constraints did Jesus have to overcome in order to free us from sin's deadly grasp (Mark 8:31–32)?

Design or Solution, Effectiveness of a

Much time and effort goes into any new product before it is approved for use by the public. Effective products have been tested over and over again. As God works in the lives of those who belong to Him through faith in Christ Jesus, He strengthens us through the trials that test us, molding, shaping, and growing us into the kind of people He desires us to become. See James 1:2–4. (8.4.1.9)

• Research the development of the vaccine for the deadly disease of polio. How effective was the serum? How long did it take to produce? What, if any, breakthroughs occurred because of this vaccine? What would the world be like today if the vaccine hadn't been developed? Who was most affected by polio before the vaccine was developed? Read John 3:16, and answer the same questions regarding Jesus Christ as the cure for humanity's fall into sin.

• Research and analyze the effectiveness of Japan's bullet trains, which move large numbers of people effectively. What does it cost to run a train? Determine if this type of transportation might be a solution to the rising costs of private transportation in the United States. Read 1 John 4:1–4. What kind of testing does God ask us to do? What are we to test? What process does He ask us to use?

Data, Quantitative, Mean, Median, Mode of

Comment to students that numbers are used symbolically in Scripture. For example, 12 is the number of tribes of Israel and the number of Jesus' disciples. Throughout the Book of Revelation, the number 12 is associated with the Church. The number 144,000, which is 12 × 12, is thought to symbolize the total number of believers. (8.4.1.10)

• Read Revelation 7:1–8. What is the mean, mode, and median of the number of believers from each tribe? What is the significance of the number 12 in Scripture? Read the remainder of the chapter. Write one or two paragraphs describing the believers in heaven.

• A farmer experimented with growing larger melons. He researched all he could about growing melons and hypothesized that adding nitrate to his fertilizer would help him grow larger melons, which he could measure by weight. For the entire season, the farmer experimented with his melons. To check his data against his control group, the farmer decided he would use the mean, median, and mode of a twenty-group sample. Find the mean, median, and mode of his sample group. The data is measured in kilograms: 2.1, 1.6, 1.6, 1.2, 2.1, 3.0, 2.5, 1.5, 1.3, 1.4, 2.0, 1.9, 1.2, 1.4, 1.9 1.5, 1.6, 3.5, 3.3, 1.6. What does our ability to think and reason reveal to us about the God who created us?

• Read Matthew 13:24–30, and interpret what Jesus is saying about the kingdom of heaven.

• After having each person jump up and down twenty consecutive times, take the heart rate of fifteen of your classmates. Then find the mean, median, and mode of that data set. Which measure (mean, median, or mode) do you think most accurately describes the data set? Read Matthew 20:1–16, and interpret its meaning. What mode is common among all of the workers?

103

Description (Observation and Summary) and Explanation (Inference, Prediction, Significance, and Importance)

Science occupies a marvelous place in the education system when it stays with the observable. Problems arise when science becomes a belief system, mainly in the explanation category of the above standard. Nonbelievers leave God and all we know of His past, present, and future interactions with us out of their inference, prediction, and significance statements. Thus, scientific beliefs are only partial. Take the time to point this out to your students, many of whom will enter secular higher education arenas where they will receive subtle bias permeating the lectures, texts, and articles they will read and study. (8.4.1.11)

• Psychology, the science of human behavior, has made some interesting observations about categories of personality. Google "Meyers Briggs" or "The Big Five + personality tests" to find assessments to take. Results will tell you which category of personality you appear to be most like using the descriptors developed. Almost all adolescents enjoy this exercise. Plus, it broadens your perspective about the variety of people who look at the same event differently. Does this test tell you which group of people will be more loving than others? more wise? more aware of truth? more likely to be chosen by God to fulfill His purposes? Point out that science does not include a complete picture of reality.

• Go to your local fish market, and explain that you want a number of fish eyes for your class. Without telling your fellow students what these are, have them write careful observations based on looks, sound, texture, and smell. Ask for the significance of these objects, distinguishing between description and explanation. Tell them what they are looking at. Ask probing questions. Why did you need a bigger picture to determine significance? Why then do we need the Bible to determine significance of people, objects, or issues?

Bias and Scientific Investigations

"Scientific knowledge is subject to change as new evidence becomes available," says one particular state standard. Unfortunately, this approach is not always practiced within the scientific community. Often it takes quite a long time for scientists who have staked their professional careers on a particular theory to acquiesce to someone else's refuting new information. Too often when experiments are set up, there is a bias toward expected results, and when results turn out different than anticipated, the original question is tweaked to make the new trials turn out to support the original hypothesis. Point out any faulty science when you see it in the news in order to give students a healthy skepticism. Comment that, unlike religion, science should not and need not be rooted in a belief system. (8.4.1.12)

• Research the Korean stem cell scandal of 2006. Also research the debate raging over the discovery of stretchy tissue found inside dinosaur bones at UNC in 2006. Only God knows the ultimate truth about many aspects of His creation. In fact, Jesus calls Himself the embodiment of truth: "I am the . . . truth" (John 14:6). Notice He does not say, "I tell the truth." Talk about the difference.

• Do a couple of the common tricks you can find online or in a library book. If possible, invite a real magician to do magic tricks for the class. After this, take a hair dryer and set a Ping-Pong ball on top of it. Turn it on. The ball will stick tight to the top of the blower and not move. Explain. (Some will think it's another trick.) Did you have a bias in your explanation? Why? Today some people have a bias against miracles. Their bias against things that can not be explained by current science make miracles impossible. Can bias be bad? good? Christians believe the Bible is the truth and have a bias in that direction. Is that bad? good?

Observable Patterns and Predictions

When you look at David's prayers recorded in the Psalms, you often see this pattern: (1) recounting of God's past mighty acts, (2) praise and confidence in God's power, (3) petition, and (4) restatement of confidence (e.g., Psalm 5; Psalm 30). Observing repeated patterns in science is also true in relationships, including yours with God. Where and when has God done acts of power, wisdom, goodness, mercy, salvation, discipline, and grace for you? Writing them down on a timeline is a helpful way to recall God's hand in your life so that present actions make sense. It's also useful when they don't. (8.4.1.13)

• Lutherans have a three-year cycle of Bible readings each Sunday through the Church Year. These readings are chosen to recount significant events in the life of our God and us, His people. Through the Church Year, we recount the birth, life, death, and resurrection of Jesus over and over again. Open to the front of the hymnal assigned to find the readings. Why is it helpful to know these particular stories, letters, and truths? Scientists can find consistent patterns in nature because our God is consistent. Scientists make predictions on this basis. Christians can predict, too, with even greater accuracy. At the end of the Apostles' Creed, we make two predictions. What are they?

• Choose something that occurs in cycles like the life cycle of a specific plant or animal. Be sure you or one of your classmates chooses the life cycle of a human. Make up simple storybooks with pictures and only a few words explaining growth. On each page opposite the picture write, "What do you think will happen next?" On the final page showing the wilted plant, also write, "What do you think will happen next?" Give these to the first-grade teacher to use for Easter this year. People don't simply die and disintegrate. Jesus promises there will be life for all who believe in Him as Savior because of His life, death, and return to life.

Directions for Conducting a Procedure

What directions does Jesus give us to repeat the procedure for living under Him in His kingdom? Eighth grade is a time adolescents are often searching for solid beliefs. Have each one practice personal devotions by reading a chapter of the Gospels each morning and keeping a daily journal of thoughts and prayers. Teach this skill. Generate directions so they can repeat the procedure daily all year long. (8.4.1.14)

• Share these billboard slogans:
Let's meet at my house Sunday before the game—God
What part of "Thou Shalt Not . . . " didn't you understand?—God
We need to talk—God
That "Love Thy Neighbor" thing . . . I meant it—God
Will the road you're on get you to My place?—God
Need directions?—God
Have you read My #1 best seller?—God
Generate billboard slogans of your own.

• Individually write directions for a science procedure you've studied in a particular unit. Exchange and carry out the direction provided by a classmate. Directions are to be followed exactly as written. This activity uses humor to show the importance of detailed directions. Afterwards discuss why God doesn't give us detailed directions for all the situations in life. (God is into dependence, not independence.)

105

Observations, Confirmed, and Scientific Claims

The difficulty of being Christian is spelled out in Hebrews 11:1, 3. "Now faith is the assurance of things hoped for, the conviction of things not seen. . . . By faith we understand that the universe was created by the word of God, so that what is seen was not made out of things that are visible." As we teach science in Lutheran schools, we want to avoid the error that only what is observed and confirmed by other observations is the sole source of truth. C. S. Lewis once said that the devil's best ploy is to convince people that the demons don't exist or are only a childhood fantasy. Demons, angels, and even a ghost are mentioned in the Bible. It is rather arrogant of humans to assume that if we cannot perceive something, it does not exist (as humans did about things like the high frequencies dogs reacted to long before we recognized their existence). It seems like God consistently puts enough unexplained phenomena into our lives to keep us from thinking humans and God are equal.

When confirmation time comes, invite your pastor to your science class for a brief comparison of the word *confirmed* as used by scientists and as used by the Church. *Confirm* can be compared to *eyewitness*. An eyewitness testimony is referenced in 2 Peter 1:16, "But we were eyewitnesses of His majesty." In John 21:24, John says of himself, "This is the disciple who testifies to these things and who wrote them down. We know that his testimony is true" (NIV). The pastor might also mention martyrs, such as the apostles, who died confessing Jesus as Messiah. Ask students if a person would die for a hoax? We support the claims made by biblical eyewitnesses by our own observations. Invite parents to be on a panel to answer questions about their observations of the truth of Jesus Christ's testimony.
(8.4.1.15)

• "In the same way, let your light shine before others, so that they may see your good works and give glory to your Father who is in heaven" (Matthew 5:16). People need to observe a difference between believers and unbelievers. After Pentecost, members of the new Christian Church captured the attention of the outside world by their attitudes and actions toward one another. Around AD 200, Church father Tertullian quoted the heathen observing Jesus' followers: "See how they love one another." Do you belong to Jesus? If I were an alien observing you and a nonbeliever, what would I see different about you? Write a response explaining what you would hope to do and not do because you are Jesus' follower.
• On a bulletin board, display promises God has made to us. With your classmates, confirm any of those promises by putting your name on a sticky note next to the verse. Have a time when you and your classmates provide confirming accounts about an event or occurrence. Promises might include these:
Rest—Matthew 11:28
He is near in time of trouble—Psalm 145:18
Source of stability, store of wisdom and knowledge—Isaiah 33:6
God will work all things for our good—Romans 8:28
He will give you the desires of your heart—Psalm 37:4
Abundant blessings—Malachi 3:10
He will never leave nor forsake us—Hebrews 13:5
• Study the big bang theory, and as a class, come up with reasons why this theory is based on faith rather than observation.
• Investigate the four Gospels to see how they complement each other. How are these books of observations? How are they confirmed?

Data Accuracy in Scientific Investigations, Importance of

Accuracy is very important for teachers. After all, when you add one little *s* to the beginning of *laughter*, you end up with a very different word! Still, besides our best efforts, we cannot be completely accurate. As you teach through this standard, urge your students to have an accurate understanding of their faith, so that they can be faithful as well as proud, bold witnesses of the grace of Jesus Christ. (8.4.1.16)

• Discuss the historical accuracy of Scripture. Cite examples from secular history and archaeology that support the teachings of God's Word.
• Talk about the importance of accuracy in two regards: (1) to ensure proper results, and (2) to remain honest. Discuss ethics in science regarding reporting results. The need for strict accuracy is a demand of Law. We take comfort in the fact that we live our lives in a state of grace under the forgiveness and empowerment Jesus provides us in the Gospel.

Conclusions, Scientific, Based on Data

As teachers, we are very much aware of the importance of growth. We look for student growth in standardized tests and on report cards throughout the year. The most important growth that we can hope for though is the spiritual growth of our students. Comment on the difficulty of quantifying or measuring spiritual growth. (8.4.1.17)

• Interpret data by graphing the average attendance of worship services at your church. Once the data has been gathered and graphed, work with classmates to formulate accurate and informative statements about the data. If a cycle of low attendance can be determined, consider ways to increase attendance.
• Contact LCMS World Mission to analyze data about new converts. Use this data to plot areas of high growth of Christianity as well as areas where a greater mission emphasis is needed.

Sequences and Symmetries

As Christian teachers, we employ review and repetition a great deal. Christians understand the importance of repetition. The Christian life is said be a repeated pattern of sin, repentance, forgiveness, and new beginning. Because we wage an ongoing battle against the devil, the world around us, and our sinful human nature, we will continue this pattern until our Savior takes us home to live with Him forever in heaven. (8.4.1.18)

• One interesting place in which symmetry in design is seen is in architecture. Take your students through a tour of your church, pointing out the structure of it and explaining the symbolism of the design.
• After studying religious symbolism, have students design their own church buildings, utilizing symmetry, symbolism, and sacred geometry.
• Read Judges 2:11–19. Identify the pattern the people of Israel experienced during the years following the death of Joshua.

Data, Used to Support Conclusions, Plans, or Solutions

In our society today, we often take a person's claim at face value without checking the facts. Stress the importance of honesty and integrity. Assure students that the facts of the Bible are grounded in God's truth, which is a truth we need never doubt! (8.4.1.19)

• Explore the Christian discipline of apologetics. Find and present apologetic materials supporting confessional claims while refuting unscriptural claims.
• Use this standard as a way to discuss evolution. One of the biggest misconceptions about evolution is that it is a proven fact. However, all claims in evolution are based on assumptions and are, therefore, based on faith.

107

Scientific Findings, Evaluation, Interpretation, and Reporting of

The furrowed brow, the deep stare—you have seen that look on your students' faces before. The wheels are turning as they try to comprehend a difficult concept. One of the joys of teaching occurs when you see your students suddenly have that "Aha!" moment. Do not be afraid to show happiness in your students' achievements. We rejoice as they grow closer to their Savior, and we can rejoice in their cognitive development too. (8.4.1.20)

• Write a paper or complete a project that defends the creationist view. Present your paper to the class. As your classmates present, ask difficult, probing questions regarding the issue. The goal of this activity is to help you and your classmates grow in your ability to defend the faith.
• Investigate the Bible's authenticity through research and comparative analysis. Review the opening words of Luke 1. Luke wrote that he gathered information "having followed all things closely for some time past" (v. 3).

8.4.2   Applying Scientific Knowledge

Graphs, Interpreting Data Using

Scripture tells us that our fall into sin has given us an impossible incline to climb to reach heaven. God gave Moses the Ten Commandments (Exodus 20:1–17) as a collection of rules to follow for the climb. Those commandments put us on such a narrow vertical path that we could never even begin the climb much less reach the top. Therefore, God in Christ carries us up that slope every time we stumble and fall. Without God's intervention (John 3:16), all of the commandments in Scripture would crush us, just as a landslide crashing down a steep mountain pulverizes everything in its path. Help students to understand the positive slope that connects them to heaven through their Lord and Savior, Jesus Christ. (8.4.2.1)

• Using a slope of ¾, draw a line that passes through the origin, and identify the x and y coordinates of seven different coordinate points. Explain how to move from one point on the line to the next point on the line, using only references to the x and y coordinates. Read Matthew 4:18–22, and consider your current point of location in your walk of faith in Jesus. Where do you move next to walk that line?
• Using a slope of –½, draw a line that passes through –4 on the y axis. With words, identify the relationship between the x coordinates and the y coordinates. If you move along the line, what happens to the value of y? Is there a constant relationship between the moves? If so, explain what that relationship is. Read Proverbs 21:16, and write a paragraph explaining this Bible verse as a negative slope in our relationship with God. Identify where this slope will eventually lead us.

Mathematical Relationships, Applying

Scripture tells us that there is a simple relationship between God and His faithful followers (John 10:27–28) and that relationship provides us with all that we need for living on Earth (Luke 11:9–13) and receiving eternal life (John 6:40). It is important for our students to learn cause-and-effect relationships, especially relationships that pull them away from the path of salvation. It is also important that our students learn not to lead others astray (Luke 17:2). (8.4.2.2)

• Consider that you are going to climb to the summit of Mt. Everest (29,028 feet), and your base camp is located on a glacier at an altitude of 22,468 feet. The current temperature is –1 degree Fahrenheit. You know that as you climb higher, the air temperature will drop one degree Fahrenheit for every 106 feet of elevation. How cold will it be at the top of Mt. Everest if the daytime temperature remains a constant –1 degree Fahrenheit at your base camp? Read John 10:27–28; Luke 11:9–13; and John 6:40, and reflect on how our behavior changes

as, working through the means of grace, the Holy Spirit brings us closer to God.

• The atmospheric pressure on Earth at sea level (1 atm) is approximately 14.7 pounds per square inch. You wish to be the first to lead a scientific expedition to explore the deepest parts of the ocean. You expect to reach a depth of 5 miles on the deepest part of your dive. If pressure increases by 14.7 pounds per square inch (1 atm) for every 33 feet you descend, what will the approximate pressure be on your submersible when you reach a depth of exactly 5 miles deep? Life can sometimes put great pressure on Christians. What can we do at such times? Read Isaiah 26:1–4 and John 6:51. Think about how God is always with us, even to the end of the world.

Data, Graphs of, Showing Linear and Nonlinear Relationships

It is possible to draw a linear path through Scripture that leads us from the fall of our first parents to the fulfillment of God's plan by Jesus Christ's resurrection (Genesis 3; Luke 2; Matthew 27–28). God has drawn a straight line for us to follow and also tells us not to stray from that path and move in a nonlinear manner (Matthew 7:14). The power God's Spirit provides us through Word and Sacrament moves us to walk a straight path in obedience to God and His will. (8.4.2.3)

• On a piece of graph paper, graph the following coordinate points (-1,-3), (0, -2), (1, 0), (3, 1), (5, 3), and (7, 8). Identify the points that are linear and the coordinate points that are nonlinear. Draw a line through the linear points, and find two additional points on the line that are not listed. Read Genesis 3; Luke 2; and Matthew 27–28. Identify points in your life where by God's grace, you found yourself in line with God's saving grace.

• On graph paper draw a line that has a slope of 3 and intersects the Y axis at -2. Identify five points on the line and a point in each quadrant of the graph that is not on the line. Read Matthew 7:14, and identify a point in your life where you have strayed from the path of God's salvation. Reflect on how God has moved you back onto that path.

Investigations, Criteria for Scientific

A systematic approach to investigating God's creation helps scientists make sense of the physical forces that control our earthly lives. Stress the important role faith plays in our approach to reading and understanding of Scripture. By the Holy Spirit's power, we receive God's saving grace in Christ's death and resurrection and rely on the truth and trustworthiness of His Word. (8.4.2.4)

• List the procedures for conducting a scientific investigation, and explain the relations among the different procedures, including the importance of testing only one variable at a time. Use your method to research the Bible and identify the plan God devised to save all people. Read Matthew 4:1–11, and determine the variable that God tested for our salvation.

• Design and test an experiment involving a 12-ounce can of regular soda and a 12-ounce can of diet soda. Research the ingredients in both cans. Hypothesize whether or not there will be a difference of density based upon the data supplied

on the labels. Devise a test to determine if the densities of the two products are different. Then, examine the data of the ingredients and draw a conclusion. Record and report your findings. Read John 10:27–28 and 1 John 4:1–3, and reflect on how Christians know their Savior and are able to distinguish Him from false prophets.

Design, A System or Object

Scripture tells us that the overriding problem facing humanity is sin (Romans 3:21–31) and that God designed a plan to correct that destructive influence. Our students daily struggle with sophisticated issues for which they are not prepared. Help students learn how to narrow down scientific research to deal with only one factor at a time and to use the Bible as a standard by which they deal with individual issues. (8.4.2.5)

• Design a system that will protect an egg from breaking when it is dropped from a height of 20 feet and lands upon the ground. The entire weight of the system may be no greater than .5 kilograms. Try out your system for a time period specified by your teacher, and then prepare to demonstrate your system to the entire class. Read Romans 3:21–31, and reflect on God's design for the salvation of mankind.
• Imagine there is a great drought happening in the midwestern United States and that you have been hired by a farmer to irrigate his fields. There is a river nearby that has unpolluted fresh water that would be an ideal water source. However, the problem you face in getting the water to the farmer's fields is that the fields are two feet higher than the water level. Research irrigations systems, and devise plans for a system that you believe would work. Be sure to draw the system to scale. Reread Romans 3:21–31, and write several paragraphs comparing and contrasting God's plan for redemption with your design to save the farmer's crops.

Modification of a Product or Design

Scripture tells us that after the fall, sin changed humanity and formed a barrier that only God could overcome. Without additional alterations, all people would face eternal death and damnation. But God provided us the needed alterations (Romans 8). We need the modification that faith in Jesus provides. We cannot be saved without it. Help students explore the alterations they make in daily living, such as the way they speak, dress, and act outwardly versus the way they feel inside. Comment on the modifications the Holy Spirit continues to make in us as He works through the means of grace. (8.4.2.6)

• Research designs for making a paper airplane, and choose one that you believe will give you the longest flight possible. Construct the model, and test its flying ability. Modify the paper airplane in a manner that you believe would increase its distance. Try out your modifications, and list the positive and negative results. What did you have to give up in order to increase the distance? Reflect on the model. Read Romans 8, and think about how sin has altered us and how God overcame that alteration.
• There has been much controversy regarding medicine that helps persons with arthritis. Some of those medicines have been recalled because they increase the risk of heart attack. Research information about arthritis pain medication, and

list the consequences of using these types of pain medicine. Think about what you might do if you were in constant pain. Would you risk increasing the chance of having a heart attack to improve your daily living? Read Mark 10:17–31. List those influences that we sometimes let get in the way of our eternal life.

Decision, Advantages and Disadvantages of a

We make many decisions in our life, and these decisions shape our future. It is important that we understand the possible consequences and opposing forces as we make decisions. Eve gave in to the serpent's temptations because she listened to the serpent's words and acted on her selfish desires, and Adam chose his wife's will over God's command (Genesis 3:1–7). As you help students critically analyze data in order to form a conclusion, encourage them to make decisions in line with God's holy will. (8.4.2.7)

• Investigate the issues involved in a major conflict happening somewhere in the world. These issues may be either scientific or social. Make a list of factors influencing decisions being made on the issue, and write a comprehensive report to share with your classmates. Discuss how God would have you think and act with regard to this issue or situation. Use Bible references to support your conclusions.

• In order to demonstrate that there are both good and bad things that happen when most decisions are made, research the scientific development of atomic energy. Make a list of good things that have come from this development and a list of bad things. Hypothesize what would have happened if the decision had been made not to use nuclear energy, such as not dropping the atom bombs on Hiroshima and Nagasaki or using nuclear fuel to make electricity. Read 1 Corinthians 10:31–33, and reflect on what God would have us consider as we make decisions.

Decisions, Using Scientific Information to Make

Scripture tells us that God made a tremendous decision early in human history (Genesis 3:14–15), and it was one that would once again bring people in close eternal fellowship with God. Scripture further tells us that God made a great sacrifice for us (John 19:28–30). As you teach the importance of analyzing data to form a conclusion, stress that God's Word leads us to the conclusion that we cannot by ourselves ever reach the kingdom of heaven. (8.4.2.8)

• Make a list of the ten most important decisions that you have made in the past three or four years. These may include decisions about friends, clothes, actions with family members or other decisions that you felt were important. Identify whether or not you felt each decision was a good one. Write down two or three sentences for each decision, describing the steps that led you to make the decisions you made, such as analyzing the consequences or simply going with your feelings at the time (instinct). Read Genesis 3:14–15, and hypothesize on the meaning hidden within the words. What was God really saying to Adam and Eve as He spoke to the serpent? What decision had God made?

• Examine the scientific procedures listed in your textbook or other resource for conducting a scien-

111

tific investigation (solving a problem). Record the list, and then analyze how a conclusion is made. Against what is the data measured in forming a conclusion? Read Deuteronomy 4:3–14; John 11:25–26; and 2 Corinthians 5:15, and reflect on the conclusion God made in bringing humanity back into harmony with Him through the merits of Jesus Christ.

Planning

One of the best ways to plan ahead is to work backwards. Who do you want to be at age forty-five, thirty, eighteen? (Notice the word *who*, not *what*. We are human beings, not human doings.)

Eighth graders are at a time where the future occupies their thoughts. Introduce the concept of planning as part of what students do in conducting a science project. Where else do they do this? (when writing papers, preparing a party, going out for a sport). Ask probing questions, such as the following: Do you think about the end and figure out how to get there? Who do you want to be at age forty-five? How would you plan backwards to be that person? When our goals include the reality of eternal life, spiritual issues play a more central focus. (8.4.2.9)

• Early in the year, formulate a plan for a service project that lasts all year. Work with class leaders to list the steps and assign materials needed as well as phone contacts. One class visited a local nursing home each month to play a simple game like Yatzee. Another visited a Title One preschool and made individual kits of games and activities that they swapped each month so that every child saw new things on their visits. By investing regular time in one specific place, relationships can be nurtured and the love of Christ shared.

• Work with your class to plan an entire chapel service. Examine all the parts of a service: praise, prayer, confession, biblical readings and interpretation, and offerings. Focus on designing each so as to make it appropriate for all who attend. Consider incorporating puppets, visual litany prayers, praise songs using rhythm instruments, and audience interaction.

• As you work with classmates to plan a science experiment, mention that in Western society, people generally think in a linear manner. This is not true in all the world. In the East, people often think more in concentric circles that get smaller or larger as one thinks about something. This approach was also prominent among the people Jesus first taught. The interpretation of parables such as the lost sheep, lost coin, and lost son demonstrates this way of thinking.

Solutions and Choices, Supporting with Scientific Evidence

Often it is the people who don't think like the majority, those who learn differently and may not do particularly well in school, who see original possibilities. These folks may be God's mouthpiece for a solution that never occurred to others. Consider Jesus as a dying Messiah to save us instead of the expected military hero, and you will see God's unexpected solution. (8.4.2.10)

• Add a debate to one of your units, expanding the final pages of the text that suggest current issues. Post several Web sites that support various viewpoints. Assign at least three sides: one side being the judges who need to review some of the various opposing research along with the two opposing sides. Give students time to research, share their findings in their groups, and prepare

for the debate. Explain the procedure. In the first round, each side gives opening positions. In the second, each side rebuts the other, and in the third, each side may reiterate their argument as well as rebut. Put a time limit on each round. Why does God give us minds with which to think? Why not just hardwire the truth into us?

• Consider the process of looking at possible solutions to something and selecting the best. Extrapolate a rule for deciding the best solution to a problem. Can your rule apply to all problems in life, including spiritual ones? Why or why not?

Theories and Scientific Models, Logical Thinking Applied to

As part of an ongoing search for truth, science continually questions its theories as new information becomes available. Show this with a simple demonstration. Hold up a clear glass of alcohol. Don't say what it is. Drop in an ice cube. Ask your students why the ice cube does this. Many will say it is due to greater or lesser amounts of air in the ice cube. The assumption is that the liquid is water, which leads to a false theory. In all things scientific, Christians need to take care to hold on to what we know to be true at the outset as spoken by the one who says that He is the way, the truth, and the life. (8.4.2.11)

• Is the opposite of logical thinking illogical thinking? Or could it be creative thinking? How would you define logical thinking? Does it consider cause and effect? deduction? induction? comparative thinking? If any piece in the line of thinking is flawed, is the rest flawed? Jesus frequently pointed out flaws in the thinking of the religious order of His day such as this: "Why do you call Me good? No one is good except God alone" (Mark 10:18). Or consider His comment about which is easier—to forgive sins or tell this paralyzed man to get up, take his bed, and go home? (Mark 2:1–12). The key question is how divine thinking is different from logical thinking. Isaiah 55:9 says, "As the heavens are higher than the earth, so are My ways higher than your ways and My thoughts than your thoughts." Have students paraphrase 1 Corinthians 1:22–25.

• Examine the debate going on between creationists and evolutionists by passing a current article from www.answersingenesis.org or www.creation instruction.org and a corresponding article supporting evolution. Divide your class in half, and challenge each other to chart the logical progression in each back to the initial presumption. Look for flaws in the logic. Switch teams and examine again. Conclude with a final paper titled "Examples of Logic."

Scientists (e.g., Dalton, John; Darwin, Charles; Mendel, Gregor; Salk, Jonas)

Some of the leading scientists in the world are or have been people with disabilities. Consider that many today advocate aborting imperfect fetuses. Imagine our field of knowledge today without: Albert Einstein (Asperger's Syndrome),

• Through your interloan program at the public library, get *Great Scientists Who Believed in the Bible* by H. M. Morris and *Scientists of Faith* by Dan Graves. Assign biography reports on various scientists including the Christians Gallileo, Kepler,

Stephen Hawking (motor neuron disease), or Pythagoras (epilepsy). Find others in *Able Scientists—Disabled Persons* by S. P. Stearner. Such would be the case if disabled people were aborted, something many think is acceptable. (8.4.2.12)

Boyle, Bernoulli, Mendel, Pasteur, Fermi, and Bacon. Consider this portion of George Washington Carver's biography: Early in G. W. Carver's career, he asked God to let him view the secrets of the universe. God would reveal to him the secrets of one of His smallest creations: the peanut. Carver acknowledged God as the source of his strength and motivation. When he received the Roosevelt medal in 1939, the following phrase was written on it, "To a scientist humbly seeking the guidance of God and a liberator to men of the white race as well as the black."
• Ask your pastor to check both within your congregation and with pastors he meets in the circuit to find a scientist willing to speak to your class. Ask him or her to explain how logical thinking plays a part in daily life and work. Ask how faith plays a part too.

Careers, Science

Whenever students talk about becoming teachers, we can feel a little humbled. Make it clear to your students that they can please God in a great number of honorable careers. Stress the need for God-fearing people in the world of science. (8.4.2.13)

• Bring in Christians from scientific fields to talk to your class about their jobs, the struggles they face, the joys they have, and the ways they serve God in their daily work.
• Hold a Concordia Fair, bringing in representatives from the different campuses to discuss the science programs offered at the colleges and universities of the LCMS.

Resources, Science Investigation

In many schools, resources may be limited because the money simply isn't available. As you teach, remind yourself and your students that God in His Word gives you all the resources you need to nurture and sustain your faith. (8.4.2.14)

• Begin a research project. As part of the project, analyze the resources you need. As you gather the resources together, remember that while we may need to search for certain resources, God has given us the resources we need to grow in faith through Word and Sacrament.
• Conduct a survey for the school or church. Possible surveys could be about worship attendance, programs wanted at school, or the number of services wanted at church.

8.4.3　Using Scientific Instruments and Technology

Instruments and Tools, Safe Use of

Safety is an issue that students easily understand. Physical safety, mental safety, and emotional safety concern most eighth-grade students, even though they often act as though they are invincible. Scripture is the only sure way to help students find the safety and security they desire. Isaiah 43:1–7 instills courage that God will not forsake us even when friends and others do. Scripture also helps calms our spirit and eases our worries (Luke 12:22–27). God frees us from the sting of death (1 Corinthians 15:55–57). Help students understand that God promises to keep us safe in His love and care and finally to take us to live forever with Him in heaven. (8.4.3.1)

• Research safety rules for working in a laboratory setting. Consider yourself to be a safety inspector for the federal government's Office of Safety and Health Administration (OSHA). Go through areas in the school where labs are taught, and audit whether or not each lab has the appropriate kinds and numbers of safety devices for the types of labs being taught. Write up a report on your findings and submit it to your science teacher. Read 1 Corinthians 15:55–57 and John 3:16 to see how God has provided for our safety for all time.
• Make a list of safety devices that are in place in your school's science lab. Then, for each safety device, write up a hypothetical situation where a student gets hurt for not using the identified safety device. For each safety device, write up another version of the same hypothetical situation showing how using the recommended safety device prevented harm. Read Isaiah 43:1–7, and make a list of the ways in which God has already kept you safe from harm.

Instruments of Measurement (Rulers, Balances, Thermometers, Graduated Cylinders, Stopwatches)

Scriptures sets the standard by which God measures us (Exodus 20:1–17). He also gives us a means of looking at ourselves and our faith (Romans 12:3–8). By using scientific measurements and standards understood by all scientists, we are able to communicate great amounts of data to scientists throughout the world. Through His holy Word, God communicates His standard, His measure, for our salvation (John 14:6) and His measure for true healing (Isaiah 53:5) that heals better than any medicine of this world (Matthew 9:1–7). (8.4.3.2)

• Using your textbook or other resource, identify which scientific instrument and what metric measuring unit would be used to collect the following data: the length of a football field, the volume of a rectangular fish tank, the mass of a small rock, the temperature of a glass of water, the volume of a child's rectangular sandbox, and the size of a red blood cell. Read Leviticus 19:2, and record the measuring tool by which God will measure us.
• Take a short walk around your school's playground area. Collect three small rocks and a piece of wood. Take the collected items into the classroom or laboratory, and find the density of each item. Density is found by dividing the mass of the object by the object's volume. Read Romans 12:3–8, and see how God measures part of our spiritual density.

Magnifying Instruments (Lenses, Microscopes, Telescopes)

As teachers we often feel like we are constantly under a microscope, constantly analyzed for any little mistake that we make. Explain to your students that Christians are often viewed with close scrutiny. Although we are not perfect, we can thank God that He sent Jesus to pay for our sin and imperfections. (8.4.3.3)

• Microscopes, telescopes, and other magnifying lenses give us the impression of being close to an organism or object. Take comfort in the fact that out Savior is always close to us. We don't need any magnification for that! Through what means does our Savior remain close to us? See John 8:31.
• Microscopes allow us to inspect something up close. When we do that to Scripture, it is called exegesis. Choose a verse on which to perform an exegesis. Use concordances to find parallel verses; Bible dictionaries and atlases will give more background information about the words used and the date and place of writing.

Calculators and Computers, Data Using

Calculators and computers are excellent tools that help us fathom and figure all sorts of equations. There is no calculation or equation that can help us figure God's love for us. Remind your students that God's love for us is so great that we can't put a price or number on it. (8.4.3.4)

• Learn about Internet safety. Identify and list safe Web sites as well as some of the ways to avoid danger and the resources that are available for Christians.
• Develop Web pages that explain the Christian faith and have links to other Christian sites.

Careers, Science

As children, we were told that we could be whatever we wanted to when we grew up. That saying is even more true for our students than it was for us! Reaffirm to your students that they can please God in church-work professions as well as in other careers. We need godly people in all walks of life. (8.4.3.5)

• Choose a scientific career to investigate. If possible, shadow a worker in that field for a day. Report to the class what you learned about the career. As part of the project, analyze how you could share your faith in your work in that field or career.
• Contact ICR (www.icr.org) and the Concordia universities to find out what careers are available for you as a Christian in the field of science. If possible, arrange to visit a Concordia to speak with professors from the science department.

Inventions, Benefits of

We can't imagine lives without computers, cars, cellular phones, and other seemingly indispensable items. In ten or twenty years, we will probably add a few items to that list. Remind your students that God is changeless and that He is truly all we need. (8.4.3.6)

• After studying simple machines and how they work, design a mousetrap utilizing these machines. If possible, construct your own mousetrap. After demonstrating and explaining what you have made, reflect that conversion through the Holy Spirit can often involve many machines. Brainstorm different elements used by the Holy Spirit to call people into God's kingdom (e.g., the Bible, pastors, a personal tragedy, friends, a letter from a believer).

• Many recent inventions are meant to aid in communication. Describe how Christians can utilize the newest technology to help spread the Gospel.

Technology Choices and Constraints

The Internet has become a great resource and yet a great curse. For every good, educational Web site out there, we always seem to find at least one bad one to match. Encourage your students in good stewardship habits and practices, and stress sanctification in their Internet decisions. (8.4.3.7)

• Identify an organization that distributes computers to families that cannot otherwise afford them. If possible, donate to the organization or hold a drive to collect old but still usable computers that could be used by the less fortunate. Such an act would be good stewardship by reusing a resource.

• If possible become classroom pen pals with students overseas. Missionaries often teach in schools and will be willing to set up the process. As part of their pen-pal relationship, find out the availability of technology in the other country. Remember to thank and praise God for the opportunities we have here in our nation.

INDEX